The Expert's Historian

The Expert's Historian

Otto Hintze and the Nature
of Modern Historical Thought

LEONARD S. SMITH
Foreword by R. Guy Erwin

◆PICKWICK *Publications* • Eugene, Oregon

THE EXPERT'S HISTORIAN
Otto Hintze and the Nature of Modern Historical Thought

Copyright © 2017 Leonard S. Smith. All rights reserved. Except for brief quotations in critical publications or reviews, no part of this book may be reproduced in any manner without prior written permission from the publisher. Write: Permissions, Wipf and Stock Publishers, 199 W. 8th Ave., Suite 3, Eugene, OR 97401.

Pickwick Publications
An Imprint of Wipf and Stock Publishers
199 W. 8th Ave., Suite 3
Eugene, OR 97401

www.wipfandstock.com

PAPERBACK ISBN: 978-1-4982-8161-4
HARDCOVER ISBN: 978-1-4982-8163-8
EBOOK ISBN: 978-1-4982-8162-1

Cataloging-in-Publication data:

Names: Smith, Leonard (Leonard Sander), 1932–2013. | Erwin, Guy.

Title: The expert's historian : Otto Hintze and the nature of modern historical thought / Leonard Smith ; foreword by R. Guy Erwin.

Description: Eugene, OR: Pickwick Publications | Includes bibliographical references.

Identifiers: ISBN: 978-1-4982-8161-4 (paperback). | ISBN: 978-1-4982-8163-8 (hardcover). | ISBN: 978-1-4982-8162-1 (ebook).

Subjects: Historiography. | Hintze, Otto, 1861-1940.

Classification: DD86.7 H56 S62 2017 (print) | DD86.7 (ebook)

Manufactured in the U.S.A.   03/20/17

Dedicated to the children of Leonard and Sharon Smith:
Eric, Kirk, Sander, and Kirstin

Contents

Foreword by R. Guy Erwin | vii
Preface | xiii
Acknowledgments | xix
Abbreviations | xxi

1 A Fifty-Year Encounter with Otto Hintze and Historicism as a Method of Doing History, 1962–2012 | 1

2 Meinecke, Troeltsch, Hintze, and the Discovery of Historicism as a Methodology | 34

3 Otto Hintze and Max Weber: From the Roots of Bureaucracy to the Invention of Historical Ideal Types | 61

4 Frederick C. Beiser and The German Historicist Tradition: A Critical Review | 80

Appendix: Inaugural Speech of Mr. Hintze | 91

Epilogue: Teaching the Idea of History and Historicism as a Method for Writing a History Paper | 95

A Typology of Western Historiography | 100
    An Ideal Type or Model of Classical Historiography | 100
    An Ideal Type or Model of Christian Historiography | 101
    An Ideal Type or Model of Modern Historiography | 102
    Quotations for a Typology of Western Historiography | 103

Bibliography | 107

Foreword

LEONARD S. SMITH'S FINAL book, *The Expert's Historian: Otto Hintze and the Nature of Modern Historical Thought*, is both a discrete collection of reflections on the development of historiography and, in the collective, a kind of intellectual autobiography. In a striking way, Dr. Smith's own development as a historian and historiographer relates to his subject matter, and this consonance adds unexpected passion and depth to his conclusions. It is not common, in the rarefied air of historiographical writing, for a historian to make a "confession of faith" in his material and his method, but Dr. Smith does just that. And anyone who knew him personally found this blend of broad and dispassionate knowledge with intense and passionate conviction to be fully characteristic of Leonard Smith the scholar, teacher, and Lutheran.

I first encountered Leonard Smith when I joined the faculties of history and religion at California Lutheran University in the year 2000. By then Dr. Smith had retired, but even as emeritus professor of history he played a prominent role in the university's wider circle of friends and supporters. He took a particular interest in me from the time of my first interview, because of our shared experience of study and research in Germany, our commitment to Lutheranism, and our common interest in Leopold von Ranke. I was honored to be in close conversation with Dr. Smith for the last dozen years of his life, and there is not much in his late work that we did not discuss. He was tenacious in his defense of his conclusions, but always open to new evidence and information, and he welcomed new angles of approach to his work—in short, he was learned and imaginative at the same time.

The community of American scholars interested in the great German historians of the late nineteenth and early twentieth centuries has never been large, and Leonard Smith was at the center of them for most of his career. In the small liberal arts college (and later university) at which he

FOREWORD

taught for most of his career, Smith was responsible for most of European history, and only his most advanced students benefited from his deep scholarship in historiography. But he prepared some of them for graduate study in that way, and many of his former students remember the intensity of his historiographical seminars with a mix of nostalgia and awe. Only at professional meetings was Smith able to connect with peers who shared his interests, and even there, the gradual eclipse of intellectual history in the 1970s onward made it somewhat challenging for him to find an audience for his work on Ranke, Hintze, Meinecke, Troeltsch, and Weber.

Most challenging of all for Smith's work was the relative indifference of historians to the religious roots of the German historians of the nineteenth century, admittedly an age of disenchantment and secularism in the face of the rise of economic theory. Smith's lifelong argument that the moderate rationalism of eighteenth- and nineteenth-century German Lutheranism—and the view of political and social reality taught through Luther's *Small Catechism* in German schools and by German pastors—actually undergirds the *Weltanschauung* of Ranke and the first generation of professional historians, was an idea that seemed old-fashioned at first, but has stood the test of time. Unfortunately Smith's thesis, presented most fully in his *Religion and the Rise of History: Martin Luther and the Cultural Revolution in Germany, 1760–1810* (2009), has not yet provoked the kind of research and analysis that could test, expand, or challenge it, but that may well be yet to come as the winds of academic fashion continue to blow in new directions.

Certainly, the recent rise in interest in Otto Hintze as a historian vindicates Leonard Smith's long fascination with his work, described in this volume's first essay. As a historian, Hintze stood in a liminal period: his early work on the Hohenzollern dynasty, easily understood as special pleading in support of an authoritarian regime, is now appreciated for the quality of its research instead of being dismissed as an artifact of pre-war monarchist propaganda. Hintze was a student of the past, much of whose work was forged in a tumultuous present: the brief creative window of the Weimar Republic. His analysis cannot be completely divorced from his lived experience—precisely the argument Leonard Smith makes about him and about Ranke as well. And the same might be said of Smith himself, whose own historical contribution spanned the drama of the Cold War era and the decline in the West of the authority and influence of traditional institutions like church and academy. Historians may write about what they find, but they write it in contexts that shape and influence how and where they have looked.

In the second essay in this volume, Smith takes the reader more deeply into the intellectual context of Hintze's work, embedding him in the golden age of German historiography together with his contemporaries and peers Friedrich Meinecke and Ernst Troeltsch. Smith evokes the heady political and nationalistic spirit that pervaded German historiography and history of political institutions in the early twentieth century.

On a more theoretical level, the third essay explores the connections between Hintze and Max Weber, and charts Hintze's use of Weber's sociological understandings and his movement beyond Marxist theories of structure. In developing his own ideas of the structures of human community, Hintze both drew from and further refined the dominant ideas of his time. Smith's appreciative essay gives us a hint, as well, of Smith's own adaptive skill in using but expanding frameworks and categories.

In the fourth essay, Smith returns to the basic idea of "historicism" as expressed by Friedrich Meinecke and described in Frederick Beiser's book *The German Historicist Tradition: A Critical View*, critiquing Beiser's interpretation from a historical perspective. The intellectual principles that Meinecke described as *Historismus* reflect an application of the great currents of German philosophy to the subject matter of history: a movement from the individualizing efforts of historical research (which digs downward into cases) to a grander framework in which the human forces in history can be understood in more general ways. In this essay, Smith also shows his rhetorical skill as he exposes several of Beiser's views to criticism based on his own deep research.

Ultimately, this volume is Leonard Smith's "confession of faith" in the historical method and analytical insight of Otto Hintze. And, characteristically, Smith lets Hintze have (almost) the last word by including his own translation of Hintze's inaugural address to the Prussian Academy of Sciences in 1914. In this speech, Hintze points frankly (and in an eerily prescient way) to the "problem of the origin of absolutism and its creature: the modern militaristic great state." Within months, the "great state" in question (and Hintze's homeland) would help plunge Europe into the vast destruction of the First World War. In that war's aftermath, Hintze will write two volumes trying to come to terms with its meaning, and ultimately, the rise of Nazism will silence his voice completely.

Foreword

Leonard Smith lived a scholar's life within a teacher's vocation. As the epilogue of this book indicates, his research was strongly reflected in his teaching. This is another illustration of Smith's thoroughness and insight that each aspiring historian needs clarity about what she is doing and what premises she is bringing to bear on her interpretation. With charm and lucidness, Smith invites his students into a conversation with the great historians of the past, to help them understand their own preconceptions and step outside of them.

"The Expert's Historian" is more than the title of Leonard Smith's final book; it is an apt description of the man himself. Perfectly at home both in the library and the classroom, Smith worked long and hard outside the limelight of historical fashion to create a lasting contribution to his field, and to build his own memorial in the hearts of his students and many friends. May his memory be a blessing!

R. Guy Erwin, PhD

Preface

IN THE YEAR 1941, Friedrich Meinecke (1862–1954)—the most famous and influential German historian of the twentieth century—summarized the significance of his friend Otto Hintze (1861–1940) for the discipline called history in this way: "As we hoped, Hintze's further development made him one of the great ones in the discipline. To be sure, he was one of those who was only known in the circle of experts, like a very high mountain in a mountain range which one first noticed from the vantage point of a high pass" (F. Meinecke, *Erlebtes*, 158–59).

In the year 1967, my PhD dissertation, "Otto Hintze's Comparative Constitutional History of the West" (Washington University, St. Louis, Missouri) was completed and became available through UMI Dissertation Services. For many reasons this was a very long dissertation (617 pages), but one of the major reasons was the necessity of summarizing many of Hintze's most important essays, since almost nothing of his work had been translated at this time. In the year 1970, in a very important essay called "Otto Hintze: His Work and Significance in Historiography," Dietrich Gerhard called attention to my dissertation and the need for it to be published in a condensed form.[1]

In the year 1975, Felix Gilbert translated, edited, and introduced some of Hintze's articles in a very important book for the English-speaking world called *The Historical Essays of Otto Hintze: Edited with an Introduction by Felix Gilbert with the assistance of Robert M. Berdahl* (New York: Oxford University Press, 1975). In the first paragraph of the "Introduction, Otto Hintze 1861–1940," Gilbert wrote: "Those acquainted with the work of Otto Hintze are unanimous in regarding him as one of the most important, if not the most important, German historical scholar of the period of William II

---

1. Gerhard, "Otto Hintze: His Work and Significance in Historiography," 74.

PREFACE

and the Weimar Republic. Yet, the number of those to whom his writings are known is small; and his influence on historical scholarship, although profound and decisive in individual cases, has been limited. Hintze's fame has certainly not reached far beyond the German frontiers" (p. 4).

In the next paragraph, Gilbert rightly explained that the "foremost reason has been the inaccessibility of Hintze's writings." This however, does not explain why this book, which Oxford University Press published both in hardcover and paperback and went all out to publicize, was a costly failure in sales. Certainly, the neglect of this book of essays by "one of the most important historians of the twentieth century" and this book of translations by Felix Gilbert, a Meinecke student who became one of the most prominent American historians of the second half of the twentieth century, suggests that this neglect is still a major problem for the entire history profession in the United States. Even today, most professional historians in the United States are not familiar with Hintze's work and his significance for Western historical thought and their profession as a whole.

One reason for this is that there is still no basic work, either in German or in English, which deals with Otto Hintze's life, work, and significance as a whole. Sadly, my long dissertation from the year 1967 is still the only single study that has attempted to do this. If, however, I would have been able to write a highly condensed and updated version of my dissertation, what publishing company would publish such a work when so few historians, history teachers, and other scholars were willing to buy such a work when they don't even recognize Hintze's name? Was there another way to make his name known in the United States first?

In 1971, when I was pursuing my study of Leopold von Ranke for a highly condensed (less than 300 pages) and updated version of my dissertation on Hintze, I discovered a quotation from Ranke written in the year 1828 that ultimately led to a book entitled *Religion and the Rise of History: Martin Luther and the Cultural Revolution in Germany, 1760 – 1810* (Eugene, Oregon: Cascade Books, 2009). Because of the title, depth, and breadth of this study, I believed that this was the best way to make Hintze's name known to a large audience, for it was an interdisciplinary work that placed him in the context of "the idea of history" or Western historical thought as a whole.

It did this first of all because *Religion and the Rise of History* was the first study to apply the ideal-type or model-building methodology of Otto Hintze to the idea of history. The work as a whole was based on three succinct and useful models for seeing and teaching classical, Christian, and modern professional historiography. Thus, this work provided the first historical typology of Western historical thought, a typology that culminated in Hintze's work and that was modeled on his complete typology of Western institutional history: feudalism, estates structure, and the modern state.

Secondly, this was the first work to suggest that in addition to his well-known paradoxical, *simul*, or "at-the-same-time" way of thinking and viewing life, Martin Luther also developed a way of teaching, preaching, and writing that was deeply incarnational, active, and dynamic and that I called an "in, with, and under" way. Together these two ways of thinking strongly influenced Leibniz, Hamann, Herder, and Ranke and therefore was a matter of considerable significance for the rise of a distinctly modern form of historical consciousness (commonly called "historicism") in Protestant Germany.

Thirdly, *Religion and the Rise of History* was the first work to suggest a new period term for seeing and teaching the formative age of modern German thought, culture, and education: "The Cultural Revolution in Germany, 1760 to 1810." This age, I claimed, began in the early 1760s and culminated in 1810 with the founding of the University of Berlin, the first fully "modern" and "modernizing" university.[2]

This university first became the recognized center for the study of history in the world, however, primarily through the work of Leopold von Ranke (1795–1886). In a chapter called "From a Holy Hieroglyph to a *Wissenschaft*[3] Alone: History as a Calling and a Profession from Ranke to Hintze," I showed how Ranke is the best example in Western literature for how a calling became a profession and how Ranke's thought was greatly influenced by Luther's two ways of thinking and viewing life. In the final section of this chapter, "Otto Hintze and the Demystifying of the Rankean View of History," I emphasized how the three-way discussion of Ernst Troeltsch (1865–1923), Otto Hintze, and Friedrich Meinecke concerning the nature of "historicism" was not only the beginning of this huge, greatly significant, and still ongoing debate today over this term but also a significant part of what H. Stuart Hughes called *Consciousness, Society and The*

---

2. Smith, *Religion and the Rise of History*, 197, and Nipperdey, "Preussen und die Universität," 144.

3. Most of the time this word is not translated here, but the usual translation is "science." In Germany, however, the word "*Wissenschaft*" is used for any organized body of knowledge with its own methodology. See, especially, L Smith, *Religion and the Rise of History*, 102, 105–07, 116–17, 120–125.

Preface

Reorientation of Western Social Historical Thought, 1890 – 1930 (New York: Vintage, 1961).

Despite the facts that Friedrich Meinecke was the only professional historian of this "generation of the 1890s" who was included in my book Religion and the Rise of History and that Hintze's name was not mentioned in its title, I used this magnificent intellectual history as a framework for showing the significance of Otto Hintze and his work. In the present study, however, this framework is part of the title.

During the 1980s and early 1990s, I started to work on my long-time dream and divided Chapter Two of my dissertation into six main traditions of nineteenth-century German historiography and had updated each of these chapters so that they could be published. However, by the late 1990s I had decided to put this project on hold until *Religion and the Rise of History* and a related essay *Martin Luther's Two Ways of Viewing Life and the Educational Foundation of a Lutheran Ethos* (Eugene, Oregon: Pickwick Publications, 2011) were published.

In May and June, 2012, however, I wrote an entirely new preface and introduction to the current study and completely changed its nature and contents. I decided that I did not have time to complete a 300-page condensation of my dissertation. Secondly, my dissertation is still a very useful source of information on Hintze for history teachers and students. In particular, my dissertation, *The Historical Essays of Otto Hintze* that were translated by Felix Gilbert, my *Religion and the Rise of History*, and this study—*The Expert's Historian*—together, would provide sufficient information and a library base for Hintze to be included in every undergraduate and graduate course in historiography in the United States. If Hintze could be included, as he should be, as one of "the great ones in the discipline" in historiography classes throughout the United States, this could greatly widen "the circle of experts" in this and other English-speaking countries and/or encourage history teachers to lead students to reach "the vantage point of a high pass" where they could see this "very high mountain" for themselves.

Although the present study, like my other books, is written for a general reader, the main audience that I have in mind here is all those college and university professors and students who participate in a seminar on historiography. Thus, for example, each reader will find a special emphasis on the importance of seminars on historiography, both for my training as a professional historian in my introductory chapter; and for teaching Hintze's

PREFACE

definition of the term "historicism" as a method for teaching students how to write a history paper, and for "doing history" in my "Epilogue." If there is another professional historian in the United States, or anywhere else, who has used or is using Hintze's understanding of historicism as a method for teaching students how to do history, I would like to meet him or her; for it is especially in this area that Hintze's reorientation of Western historical thought is still an ongoing need and process. This is what this book is about.

This book is unique both in form and content. While chapters two and three—"Meinecke, Troeltsch, Hintze and the Discovery of Historicism as a Methodology" and "Otto Hintze and Max Weber: From the Roots of Bureaucracy to the Invention of Historical Ideal Types"—are each intellectual histories focusing on one of Hintze's greatest contributions to the idea of history, chapters one and four are very different in both form and content.

Chapter one is an introduction to the literature of Otto Hintze through an autobiographical essay called "A Fifty-Year Encounter with Otto Hintze and Historicism as a Method of Doing History, 1962–2012." The fourth chapter is a completely different kind of essay, for it is a critical review of Frederick C. Bieser's *The German Historicist Tradition*, a very important book especially for what he calls the "Anglophone reader," "the Anglophone world," and "an Anglophone audience."

These are new and useful terms for me that can be applied to all my work as a professional historian, for they signify not only the English-speaking world, but also a reader and an audience whose first language isn't German. This is the audience and world that I have been trying, very unsuccessfully, I might add, to reach for more than fifty years.

Two very important parts of this book are the two added attachments. The first is "The Inaugural Speech" that Hintze gave to the Royal Prussian Academy of Sciences in Berlin in 1914, a key for understanding his goals and work as a whole and a document that is translated into English here. The second attachment is an "Epilogue" that no historian has ever done before, for it is a four-part classroom presentation called "Teaching the Idea of History and Historicism as Method for Writing a History Paper." The main part of this epilogue is the classroom presentation that I gave to first-year college and university students every semester at California Lutheran University for about twenty years—a presentation that I called "Historicism as a Method of Teaching Students How to Write a History Paper." While one of the parts was a two-sided sheet called "A Typology of Western Historiography," a typology that contains succinct and useful

Preface

"ideal types" or models for seeing and teaching classical, Christian, and modern professional historiography, another part was a two-sided sheet containing three quotations from each of these three main periods. While the three ideal types have been published before (since they provided the basic structure of my study *Religion and the Rise of History: Martin Luther and the Cultural Revolution in Germany, 1760–1810* (2009), the other parts have never before been published.

This Preface is also unique, for instead of thanking all the persons who have assisted me in the research and writing of this book (as I did in the above mentioned book), I want to use this opportunity to thank the four persons to whom this work is dedicated—the four children of Leonard and Sharon Smith. That is, Eric (b. 1960), Kirk (b. 1962), Sander (b. 1964), and Kirstin (b. 1971). One reason that I need (and hopefully will be able) to complete this study is that my wonderful wife, who is now also my full-time caregiver, rightly insists that I owe them this. I owe them this because for the earliest years of our three boys, their father was a graduate student doing research on his dissertation and seldom had time for them.

For example, I first met my son, Sander, at the end of August, 1964, since my wife and first two sons flew from Germany to her home in Bismarck, North Dakota in April so that she could have our baby in the United States (June 7) and so that I could do my needed research in East and West Berlin and in Merseburg, East Germany during the summer months. Later, when our boys and our daughter were growing up, I was gone for months at a time for sabbatical leaves back to Germany for more research on what the family always called "Dad's book."

Acknowledgments

WITH THE PASSING OF my late dear husband, Leonard S. Smith (August 8, 2013), it fell willingly and with love to the family, to read my husband's last manuscript and to prepare it for publication. Once we felt the manuscript was "ready," we gave it to our good friend, the Rev. R. Guy Erwin PhD, who had promised Leonard that he would read his manuscript from a professional standpoint before releasing it to a publisher. The first "Thank-you" goes to sons Eric and Sander who helped me "clean it up," citing errors and noting concerns and secondly, to Dr. Erwin, who since making that promise to Leonard, became "Bishop" R. Guy Erwin. He reminded me that he hadn't forgotten his promise to Leonard and has indeed completed that task. He also agreed to write the "Foreward."

Thank you Bishop Erwin!

Two others played a role in this manuscript. Leonard wanted to place in an "Appendix," the speech that Otto Hintze presented to the "Royal Prussian Academy of Sciences." However, I could not find his translation of it. I found the reference for it in a text written by Otto Hintze and presented copies to each of two people who knew the German language—Ernst F. Tonsing PhD, Professor Emeritus of the Religion Department at California Lutheran University; and Nancy Truex PhD, German Scholar and Language Instructor. Both of their transcripts were given to Bishop Erwin, who with knowledge of this language as well, could make the final decision as to which, or a combination of all three, was the best translation of this speech.

Thank you Dr. Tonsing and Dr. Truex!

Miracle of Miracles, my son Sander went carefully through many files and found Leonard's translation which, of course is the one that is used.

Acknowledgments

Pictures always add a special element to anyone's published text. The personal family of Otto Hintze has played a key role in providing original pictures of both Otto Hintze and his wife Hedwig.

Our most sincere thanks to the Hintze Family!

Lastly, I want to say a very special "Thank you" to my son, Sander, who made all the corrections that were found as we read the manuscript and did all the computer work in sending it to Wipf and Stock for publication. From your whole family, Sander,

Thank you Sander A. Smith!

We hope you, the reader, will enjoy this work and the information regarding the development of history as an academic discipline. It is our fervent wish that it can be useful to scholars in the discipline, as well as enjoyable. We hope that the publication of his last work reaches students, teachers of history, and scholars throughout the world who have an interest in how "History" became an academic discipline and a profession. Everything has a history as to how it came to be and in this case, Otto Hintze played the key role, among others, in defining "History" as an academic discipline.

Abbreviations

GA I. Hintze, Otto. *Staat und Verfasssung: Gesammelte Abhandlungen zur allgemeinen Verfassungsgsgeschichte.* Edited by Gerhard Oestreich. Göttingen, Vandenhoeck & Ruprecht.

GA II. Hintze, Otto. *Soziologie und Geschichte: Gesammelte Abhandlungen zur Sociologie, Politik und Theorie der Geschichte.* Edited by Gerhard Oestreich. Göttingen, Vandenhoeck & Ruprecht.

GA III Hintze, Otto. *Regierung und Verwaltung: Gesammelte Abhandlungen zur Staats-, Rechts-, und Sozialgeschichte Preussens.* Edited by Gerhard Oestreich. Göttingen, Vandenhoeck & Ruprecht.

HZ. *Historische Zeitschrift*

Schmollers Jahrbuch. *Jahrbuch für Gesetzgebung, Verwaltung, und Volkswirtschaft.*

1

A Fifty-Year Encounter with Otto Hintze and Historicism as a Method of Doing History, 1962–2012

Hintze's further development, as we hoped, made him one of the great ones in the discipline [*Wissenschaft*]. To be sure, he was only known in the circle of experts, like a very high mountain in a high mountain range which one first notices from the vantage point of a high pass. To me, when I think about Hintze's place in the discipline, I always picture the beautiful *Geisterspitze* in the Ortler district, which one cannot see from the valley. He was always too proud to make it easier for the world to approach his work.

—Friedrich Meinecke (1941)[1]

There is no doubt that with the perspective which only the passage of time provides, Hintze emerges as the most important figure in German historical scholarship in the twentieth century.

—Felix Gilbert (1947)[2]

    1. Meinecke, "Erlebtes," 158–59. In my shorter citation and translation of this important passage in *Religion and the Rise of History*, the words "a very high mountain" were inadvertently left out.
    2. Gilbert, "German Historiography," 52–53.

The Expert's Historian

In the beginning, was Professor Dietrich Gerhard (1896–1985), for he was the international teacher and scholar who helped me select a research topic that captured my life as a scholar for fifty years. While most of the present study is based on my dissertation, "Otto Hintze's Comparative Constitutional History of the West" (Washington University, St. Louis, Missouri, 1967), this chapter is the story of the making of my dissertation; my "sticking to this topic" in relation to the literature on Otto Hintze (1861–1940) to the present; and to this book as a whole, including its very pedagogical "Epilogue."

Helping a student in picking a topic, in focusing his or her research, in telling a good story, and then in writing a good paper or thesis, are four of the most important things that historians get paid to do. For me, Professor Dietrich Gerhard was not only the best trained and knowledgeable professional historian that I have known; he was also the best possible person to introduce me not only to Otto Hintze but also to German historiography as a whole.

In 1914, just after the outbreak of World War I, Dietrich Gerhard enrolled at the University of Berlin and in Hintze's course on *Politik,* which in that semester was called *Allgemeine Staatslehre auf historischer Grundlage (Politik).*[3] Half way through this course however, he volunteered for service in the German army, and when he returned to this university in 1919, Hintze was no longer teaching. Here he was superbly trained especially in the seminars of Friedrich Meinecke (1862–1954), probably the most famous and influential seminars in the field of history in the world during the 1920s.[4] Like other Meinecke students, Gerhard often attended the famous "Hintze teas" that Hedwig Hintze (1884–1942, also a Meinecke student) arranged for her husband. From 1932 to 1935, Gerhard was a "Private Lecturer" or an Assistant Professor at the University of Berlin, and from 1935 to 1936, he was a guest professor at Harvard University.

From 1936 to 1966, Dietrich Gerhard was a Professor of History at Washington University in St. Louis, and from 1961 to 1967 he also taught one semester each year as an Honorary Professor of American Studies at Göttingen University. At the same time while he was teaching American history at this university, he also served as the Director of the Department

---

3. "General Political Theory on an Historical Basis (Politics)."

4. See, especially, the references to the significance of Meinecke's seminars in Lehman and Sheehan, eds., *An Interrupted Past: German-Speaking Refugees in the United States after 1933,* for here Meinecke, his students, and his seminar are cited throughout this book. See also Gilbert, *A European Past: Memoirs 1905–1945,* 68–76.

of Modern History at the Max-Planck-Institute for History, a research institute that was also located in Göttingen. Thus, when I was taking courses as a PhD candidate at Washington University (1960–62), and when—with his great assistance—I became a Fulbright student at Göttingen University (1962–64), I took courses from him both in English and in German. And through Professor Gerhard's assistance, during the two academic years that the Smith family of four lived in Göttingen, I had a place to work and do my research at this wonderful institute.

Before I first met Professor Gerhard, I could read and understand (but not write) German, for as an undergraduate I had taken three years of German. And as a draftee soldier in Germany (1955–56), I had learned to understand and speak the language (but not correctly). In addition, when I was a MA candidate at the University of Iowa (1957–58), I had taken an excellent course in Modern German History, as well as a course in Modern Russian History from Nicholas Riasanovksy.[5]

At the time I first met Professor Gerhard, I had taught a year-long course in European history as an instructor at Luther College in Decorah, Iowa (1958–60); I had received a very generous fellowship from Washington University to begin working on a PhD in history; and I had first encountered the chair of the History Department at Washington University and a whole new kind of history seminar.

When I reported in at the History Department office at the beginning of the fall semester 1960, the office secretary informed me that Professor Jack Hexter, the chair of the department, had instructed her to inform me that he expected me to enroll in his seminar on Tudor and Stuart England. Since I had been a soldier for two years of my life, I knew an order when I received one, and so I registered for this three-hour course. I had received my professional training primarily from Professor Gerhard and secondly from Professor Hexter, and both of them deeply influenced the way that I taught and wrote history. Since both of them shaped what I have to say

---

5. Both of these courses were taught during my first semester (the spring of 1957) and Professor Riasanovsky's last semester at this university, and both of these courses had a lasting influence on my teaching career. In his tests, for example, he always included terms to identify, a short essay, and a main essay asking each student to "Outline and discuss the development of . . ." This is the format that I used throughout my teaching career, for here he was teaching each student how to think historically. During this semester he was working on the text that became a standard one in the field of Russian history for many years, and during my teaching career, I used every edition of this text in a course that I taught every other year.

The Expert's Historian

in my "Epilogue," it is necessary to say something about this second great scholar/teacher for this story.

Professor Jack Hexter was an imposing professor, and his opening statement to his seminar I will never forget. "This seminar," he said as he looked directly at me, "has one purpose. Some people can write history and some can't. We are here to find out who can and who can't." Then he briefly described how this was a two-semester course; how the first was an "undergraduate type seminar" consisting of several brief and duplicated papers that would introduce us to the field of Tudor–Stuart England; and how the second semester would be a strictly graduate-type seminar with one major research topic and a duplicated paper for each student. After this opening meeting, he said, this seminar would meet one evening each week for three hours in his home.

Then he asked if there were any questions. When no other students asked a question, I naively asked, "Professor Hexter, do you have any suggestions about the length of our papers?" "This seminar," he sternly answered, "is concerned with the quality of research and writing rather than the length of the paper." When no other questions were asked, he then said that his senior graduate assistant would explain to us the details that we needed to know and then departed. This was my introduction to the formidable Jack Hexter.

After he departed, his senior PhD candidate and assistant answered my question in a more helpful way. Professor Hexter, she explained, likes papers of about twelve pages in length and typed double-spaced. Each paper was to be typed on a "ditto master," "run off," and then stapled at the history department on the morning of the day before the seminar so that every participant would have a copy of each paper in time to read and discuss it. Thus, in this seminar, there was no time-consuming reading of seminar papers; the students were much more actively engaged in the discussion of each paper; and there was a much greater emphasis on writing and the craft of writing history. For me, this new type of "undergraduate seminar" became the basic one that I later introduced at two liberal arts colleges, for it was very useful for teaching both "the science" and "the art" of writing history. To me, it was also a wonderful fusion of the German research seminar and the English and American emphasis on teaching writing.

At the end of the semester, Professor Hexter explained that those students who were not planning to take the second half of the course would receive a grade, but those who would take the full course, would receive their grades for both semesters at the end of the second semester. Since he was both an excellent and rigorous seminar teacher, I signed up for the second semester. My reward for this was the research topic, "English agriculture in the sixteenth century"—a topic that I had mastered to his satisfaction by the end of the academic year 1960–61.[6]

The next year, I chose Tudor-Stuart England as one of the fields for my doctoral examination, and during my fourth semester at Washington University, I registered for an independent study from Professor Hexter to prepare for this examination. He then gave me a list of about sixty-two works (several of them two volumes) and asked me how many of these I had read. After looking at the list, I replied that I had read about half of them. "When you have read the rest of them, come and see me." After receiving an incomplete at the end of the semester, and after using most of the summer to complete this reading assignment, I presented myself to him to complete the course. "Since I will be examining you in this field as part of your doctoral examination when Professor Gerhard returns from Germany," he said, "I will give you a grade then." This was Professor Jack Hexter, the best teacher I have ever known for teaching students (and professors)[7] how to write history and the "craft" of "doing history."[8]

When I enrolled in Professor Gerhard's course in Russian history, I encountered another truly exceptional scholar and teacher. First of all, from the beginning, this course was based on a distinction between a "geographical Europe" and a "historic Europe" or a Europe that had developed out of the Latin or Western church and which had acquired both its unity and its basic institutions between 1000 and 1800.[9] A second basic emphasis

---

6. At the close of our last meeting in his home, he informed me that he had talked to a publisher about a possible article on this subject, but this would require at least the same amount of work that I had already done.

7. At Yale University, where he taught until Yale's mandatory retirement-age policy led him to return to Washington University, he offered an excellent summer seminar for the National Endowment of Humanities for professors from colleges and universities that didn't have a major research library. The course was called "Writing History," and it focused on one package of documents about a disputed election in England at the beginning of the reign of James I. It was very fortunate for me to be included in this great seminar in the year 1978, both for my writing and for the research that I was able to do in the magnificent Yale libraries for the book that later became *Religion and the Rise of History*.

8. See Hexter, *Doing History*.

9. See Gerhard's excellent and brief study called *Old Europe: A Study of Continuity and Change, 1000–1800*.

was how the whole cultural and institutional development of Russia was shaped by the fact that Russia was converted to Christianity from Constantinople rather than from Rome at about the same time that "Europe" was taking shape. Thirdly, he emphasized how the Muscovite period was basic for Russian history because it was at that time that it acquired its three basic characteristics—autocracy, serving gentry, and serfdom—and became most unlike historical Europe. These emphases shaped not only my course in Russian history but also my basic views in teaching European history since this time.

In this lecture course, like all of Professor Gerhard's lecture courses (both in the United States and in Germany), he encouraged students to ask questions. One of the most memorable and important events for me, was his answer to a student question: "Dr. Gerhard, what were the main causes of World War I?" Well, he said, for most of this war, I fought in the German army against the Russian army on the eastern front. At that time, he said, it was not called by that name. World War I is really a collective name that historians give to a number of conflicts that were fought during the years from 1914 to 1918, where nations were fighting nations for all kinds of reasons. Unlike many historians, he explained, I don't believe anyone can definitely say that this was the main "cause" or that these were the four or five "causes" of this war or of the American Civil War. In fact, he said, I don't use the word "cause" or list the "basic causes" of any great event, for life is very complex and I believe that the historian who does claim to know this is naive. More than that, to me this is playing God, for I believe that only God knows why things happen. The job of the historian, he explained, is to tell *how* something happened or *how* something came to be, and this, he said, "is good enough for me."

At Washington University, I also discovered that when I enrolled in Professor Dietrich Gerhard's historiography seminar, which also met one night a week in his home, I couldn't have found a better place to find a dissertation advisor in the field of German history. One event during this seminar that made a deep and lasting impression on me was when I mentioned that as a teacher of modern European history, I had assigned Crane Britton's *Anatomy of Revolution* as a supplementary history text. His reaction was both very interesting and totally new for me. "This is a very interesting book," he explained, "but you can't call it a history." Any book that compares the English revolution of the seventeenth century with the American and French revolutions of the late-eighteenth century and with the Russian Revolution of the early twentieth century for the purpose of establishing a pattern of revolution, he said, can be called social science but not a history; for time is irrelevant here. In contrast, he explained, R. R. Palmer's two-volume *The Age of the Democratic Revolution*, which compared the American and French revolutions within the context of a Western revolution that he named, was definitely a history; for it was solidly based on a perception of time. This was a view that was both new and very interesting for me because I had never encountered a historian before who was strongly concerned about the nature and boundaries of history as an academic discipline.

During the time of this seminar, I informed Dr. Gerhard that I wanted to do my dissertation in the field of German history and that I wanted him to be my PhD advisor. When he asked me what kind of topic I had in mind, I replied that I had no idea and that I was certainly open to suggestions. His response to this was to give me a list of names, mostly of nineteenth and early-twentieth-century German historians, and instructed me to check them out. After some time, I came back to him with the name Otto Hintze. When he asked me why I had picked him, I replied that of all the names he had suggested, I found that he was easiest for me to read and understand because his sentences were always clear. His reply to me was that I had chosen not only the most important of these German scholars but also the most difficult one to fully comprehend. "Frankly," he said, "I am not sure that you can handle him; but if he is the one that you want, let's go with him."

What I did not know at this time, however, was that since World War II, Dr. Gerhard had based his whole way of teaching on a comparative institutional approach that he had learned mainly through Hintze's writings. During this war, Washington University was a training place for future military government officers for an occupied Germany, and Gerhard became one of their main instructors. As a group, Gerhard liked to say, they were the best students he ever had, but they knew very little about European or German history. At this time, Gerhard discovered that Hintze and Alexis de Tocqueville were the two most helpful scholars in teaching these exceptional students how to understand German institutions, society, and culture within a European and Western perspective, and, at the same time, for the development of a comparative institutional way of teaching that was new and decisive for him. What Gerhard did not need to tell me, however, was something I had already learned in his unique and wonderful course on Russian history; namely, that his base for comparison was "historical individuality" or "historic Europe," which had emerged within and out of the Western or Latin Church.

It was also only after I was well into my research on Hintze that I learned that it was mainly from him that Gerhard had adopted his basic view that a history had to be based on a perspective of time; otherwise it could not be called a history. This, however, was one of the most important lessons I had already learned in Gerhard's historiography seminar. What I did not know, however, was that when I picked Hintze as my research topic, I had selected Gerhard's most important professional historian for his comparative institutional way of teaching history, for his main historical object and subject, and for his understanding of the nature of history.

The place to start on this topic, Gerhard explained after we agreed that Hintze would be the object of my research and the subject of my dissertation, is with Hintze's "Entrance Address" to the Royal Prussian Academy of Sciences in 1914. Gerhard then continued to say, "I want you to translate this address for me." This assignment proved to be very difficult, for it was not an easy document to translate, especially with my knowledge and skills at that time. It did, however, provide the three keys that I needed to begin to understand all of Hintze's work and to begin more than fifty years of research in trying "to handle" this great historian.

"From the beginning," Hintze declared in this address, "the real goal that I had in mind for my scientific efforts was a general comparative constitutional and administrative history of the states in the modern world, particularly of the Latin and Germanic nations. In this direction," he added, "I felt that the great life work of Ranke allowed for and needed supplementary work."[10]

A second key was the way he viewed the relationship between his intensive study of the Prussian state, for Hintze stated, "Prussian history would be a paradigm to me for the formation of the modern state and for the changes it underwent."[11]

The third key was contained in a shorter paragraph where Hintze introduced the second main goal of his life. To him, it was both possible and necessary "to bring the results of a comparative historical consideration of

---

10. Hintze, "Antrittsrede des Hrn. Hintze." In the 3rd edition of volume 1 of Hintze's *Gesammelte Abhandlungen* in 1970, Oestreich included this address. Since this is now the most convenient place to read this key document, future references will be to this work. Today it is translated in the Appendix of this book.

11. Hintze, "Antrittsrede," 564–65.

the political life of the modern nations into a systematic unity as historians and jurists have tried to do continually and as I have tried to do in my courses concerning *Allgemeine Staatslehre auf historische Grundlage*."[12]

The timing for the beginning of my dissertation research and my fifty-year investigation was extremely fortunate, for before the year 1962, it was very difficult to do research on Otto Hintze.[13] First of all, before Fritz Hartung (1883–1967), a Hintze student and his successor as a professor of constitutional history at the University of Berlin, first collected and published some of Hintze's very scattered articles, it was very difficult even to find them. Because of severe wartime conditions when the three volumes of Hintze's collected articles were first published (1942–43),[14] however, the number of copies was very limited, and by this time Hintze's name and work had almost been forgotten even in Germany.

This Hartung edition of Hintze's collected articles, however, first made it possible to see Hintze's work as a whole and for Felix Gilbert to assert in 1947 that "There is no doubt that with the perspective which only the passage of time provides, Hintze emerges as the most important figure in German historical scholarship of the twentieth century."[15]

The year 1962 was a turning point for Hintze research, for in that year Professor Gerhard Oestreich (a student of Hartung) edited and published a greatly enlarged first volume of Hintze's collected articles—a volume called *Staat und Verfassung: Gesammelte Abhandlungen zur allgemeinen Verfassungsgeschichte*.[16] It was a turning point not only because it included sixteen of Hintze's independent articles and essays and two previously unpublished writings out of the Hintze *Nachlass* or Papers, but also because it contained a year-by-year listing of Hintze writings (that had first been compiled by H. O. Meisner for the first edition of Hintze's collected essays), plus a listing of 248 of Hintze's book reviews from 1885 to 1933.

---

12. Ibid., 565. Originally this lecture and this goal was simply called *Politik*.

13. See, especially, Milton Covensky, "Otto Hintze and Historicism: A Study of the Transformation of German Historical Thought." It is a sad fact that this dissertation, which is still a useful introduction to Hintze and his work, is available by interlibrary loan in the United States in book form (UMI Dissertation Services) only from several academic institutions in Germany. In 1962, however, I had to buy a microfilm copy of this dissertation.

14. Hintze, *Gesammelte Abhandlungen*, 43.

15. Gilbert, "German Historiography," 52–53.

16. Hintze, *Staat und Verfassung*. Henceforth references to this volume and this edition are cited as Hintze, GA I.

From the time I arrived and enrolled as a student at Göttingen University and began working at the Max-Planck-Institute for History (October 1962), my research consisted mainly of reading all of the books, articles, essays, and book reviews that were listed at the end of this volume. Thus, by the time that my pregnant wife and two children returned to the United States (April 1964), I was sufficiently prepared to begin archival research in Berlin (both West and East) as well as in the Hintze papers in Merseburg in Communist East Germany or the German Democratic Republic (DDR).

In West Berlin, I had very little difficulty in using the library of the Free University of Berlin and the Meinecke papers in the *Geheime Staatsarchiv Berlin,* or in using the archives of the Humboldt University and the German Academy of Sciences in East Berlin. However, using the Hintze papers in Merseburg was an entirely different matter.

First of all, I knew that because of the Cold War, it was almost impossible for West German scholars to obtain permission from the Ministry of Interior of the German Democratic Republic (DDR) to use the part of the Prussian archives that was located in Merseburg. Secondly, I had been told that when Professor Oestreich had used the Hintze papers located in Merseburg, he had actually read and used them in Berlin. Thus, after I had written a formal request to the Ministry of Interior to allow me to use the Hintze papers in the German Central Archives in Merseburg and had not received a reply, I went to the Ministry of Interior and asked for this permission in person.

This experience is still very vivid in my mind, for the impressive building, the large and high ceilings of all the offices, the Spartan-like furniture, the large desks, the military uniforms, the clicking of heels, the use of the word "comrade," and the very formal language as I was passed up the chain of command, reminded me of Kafka and his great novels. Finally, after they had found my correspondence, I was informed that my request had been conditionally approved. The condition was that I first had to go to the Tourist Bureau to pay for a hotel room for each night that I would be in the DDR. After paying for a hotel room for a week in Halle (because no hotel room was available in Merseburg during that week), I returned to the Ministry of Interior to complete the process and receive a visa.

Now that I had permission to travel in the DDR, when my visa began, I immediately took the train from East Berlin and around West Berlin to reach Potsdam. By this time, I had already visited and briefly interviewed Fritz Hartung, but now I wanted to see the palace of Frederick the Great and to meet and interview Dr. Otto Meisner, a prominent Hintze student who had written a thorough and inclusive essay honoring Hintze's life and work in the *Historische Zeitschrift* shortly after his death.[17]

When I had interviewed Dr. Hartung (9/7/1964), I asked him questions about both Otto and Hedwig Hintze. With regard to Otto Hintze, Dr. Hartung confirmed what he had written in 1941 and repeated in 1964[18]—that in 1930, Hintze had informed him that his comparative constitutional history manuscript was complete and ready to be published. With regard to the "Hintze teas," Dr. Hartung indicated that for him, these teas were dominated too much by Hedwig Hintze. When I mentioned how impressed I was by Hedwig Hintze's book called *Staatseinheit und Föderalismus im alten Frankreich und in der Revolution* (1928), Dr, Hartung replied rather stiffly that she couldn't have written it without the help of her husband. Before I left however, Dr. Hartung did autograph his introductory essay—called "Otto Hintze's Lebenswerk—in my now very used copy of *Staat und Verfassung* that Oestreich had published in 1962.

When I met Dr. Meisner (11/7/1964), I was impressed with his lovely home in Potsdam, his excellent health, his joy in visiting with a young American who was doing research on Otto Hintze, and with his rather warm and positive disposition. What he regretted about his situation, however, was the difficulty of communicating with friends and scholars outside the DDR and the difficulty of obtaining books, articles, and information. Like Dr. Hartung, however, Dr. Meisner also believed that Hintze's comparative constitutional history was finished and ready to be published in 1933.

During my daily round trips from Halle to Merseburg, I experienced the most polluted air and sky that I have ever had to endure, for this small electric train took me directly through "the Leuna works," the largest area of chemical plants that I had ever seen. Each morning, after I arrived at the back door of the hospital that housed the part of the Prussian archives that I most needed, and after I had been ushered to the reading room and to my assigned table, I would request the Hintze papers that I wished to see that day. Each noon, all the readers marched together to a nearby factory for

---

17. Meisner, "Otto Hintze's Lebens Werk." This essay is especially noteworthy for Meisner's emphasis on Hintze's articles and book reviews from 1920 to1933; his ideal types; and the significance of Max Weber for Hintze at this time.

18. Hartung, "Otto Hintzes Lebenswerk."

lunch in its cafeteria, which was the only time that we had the opportunity to visit with each other.[19]

At Merseburg, I encountered the most difficult time of all my years of research, for up to this time I was dealing almost entirely with printed or typed documents. Here, however, I was faced almost entirely with handwritten documents that I could not read because they were written in the old German script that was commonly used before 1933. Fortunately, I was partly prepared for this enormous difficulty because I had with me a copied page from the *Brockhaus Encyclopedia* which showed what each letter, both small and capital, looked like. By this time, I didn't need to use a dictionary in reading Hintze's writings, but research is very difficult when one can't read the letters in each word. Thus, when I couldn't make out a particular letter in a word, I would leave an underlined blank space in my large note cards, and frequently, I had to make trips to the front desk to ask for assistance from the two young ladies who brought us our documents. Thus, it was no accident that after Germany was reunited, and after the Prussian archives were also reunited in Berlin, these two ladies and I recognized each other as they assisted me—once again—in the Prussian and German archives.

After a week of trying to decipher Hintze's handwriting, I realized that I badly needed an extension of my visa. The only two places where this could be done were Berlin or Leipzig. In Leipzig, I was able to obtain a hotel room in Merseburg and an extension of my visa for a second week. In addition to this extension of time, however, I also badly needed copies of some of the most important documents that I needed for further study. Since at this time, both I and my family in the United States were living entirely off borrowed money, both the number of photo copies and the cost per copy were a matter of grave concern to me, especially when the Director of the Archive would not inform me what the cost would be. Instead of a money payment, however, what he wanted was an exchange. The deal that he offered me was that after I received a microfilm from him at my new address in the United States, he would inform me what he wanted in exchange.

Shortly after I had resumed my teaching career again in the fall of 1964, now as an assistant professor of history at Luther College in Decorah, Iowa, I received my microfilm reel and first learned what the exchange

---

19. The one person with whom I did converse was a newly appointed full professor from the University of Aarhus in Denmark, who informed me that he was only one of four full professors in that country.

would be: a specified number of a microfilm reel from the National Archives in Washington, D.C. When I received my Hintze microfilm, both I and one of my colleagues who could read German, rushed to the college library and located a microfilm reader to see what it was that this director and the DDR really wanted: a completely full reel of documents from the office of Heinrich Himmler, a reel that contained many personnel files of his SS officers. Thus, for about ten dollars, I had received a microfilm reel that was of great value for me, and the DDR had received from me, a microfilm that they could have ordered directly themselves at the same cost.

Before I left Germany, however, I was able to meet and enjoy the great hospitality of Professor Gerhard Oestreich and his wife Brigitta in their home in Hamburg, Germany. The chief purpose of this visit for me was to see and take notes on a student manuscript of Hintze's course on comparative constitutional history that Oestreich now possessed. We also had time to discuss Hintze's work and what I had found in Merseburg.

The year 1964 was a very important year both for Professor Oestreich and for Hintze research because in that year, Oestreich published a new and greatly enlarged second volume of Hintze's collected essays and with it, a very important introductory essay to this volume. While the title of the volume was called *Soziologie und Geschichte: Gesammelte Abhandlungen zur Soziologie, Politik und Theorie der Geschichte*,[20] the title of the introductory essay was called "Otto Hintze's Relation [*Stellung*] to Political Science and Sociology." One of the reasons that this comprehensive essay was significant both for me and for Hintze scholars since then is that in the first main part of this essay, a part called "Monarchical Political Scientist," Oestreich emphasized the importance and the nature of Hintze's course on "*Allgemeine Staatslehre*" or *Politik*. From the lecture notes for this course from the year 1911 that he had received from Dr. H. O. Meisner, Oestreich listed the titles of the eight main sections and the topics that were discussed in each of these sections.[21]

While in this part of this essay, Oestreich called Hintze a "Political Scientist,"[22] in the second main part of the essay, Hintze was pictured also as an historical sociologist. Although Oestreich emphasized that Hintze was and remained a "historian and historicist" (48); that he firmly declined to consider himself to be "a sociologist thinker" (67); and that "he was and

---

20. Hintze, *Soziologie und Geschichte*. Hereafter this volume is cited Hintze, *GA II*.
21. Oestreich, "Otto Hintze's Stellung zur Politikwissenschaft und Soziologie."
22. Ibid., 13, 15, and 17.

wanted to be a historian in method and the direction of his work (67), it is significant that the title of the second main part—where he discussed Hintze's relation to Max Weber—was called "From Pragmatic Historicism to Historical Sociology" (35).

While Oestreich certainly was right when he claimed that Hintze was and remained "a historian," and that he never called himself a "historicist," a "political scientist," a "sociologist," or a "sociologist thinker," he would not have called his kind of history "pragmatic historicism." For Hintze, "pragmatic" was the term he used for political history or for the kind of history of the Greek and Roman historians whose main concern was to investigate the meaning and coherence of events in terms of the purposeful action of statesmen, military leaders, and other influential men.[23] In addition, the term "historicism" was a very disputed term and was not really used in Germany before World War I, or before the debate between Troeltsch, Meinecke, and Hintze concerning the use of the term during and especially after the war.

When I was visiting Professor Oestreich in August, 1964, he indicated to me that he didn't want me to see Meisner's lecture notes for Hintze's course called *Allgemeine Staatslehre* because he soon wanted to publish this lecture. The most interesting, memorable, and surprising part of our discussion, however, was his rather strong views concerning the relation of the terms "state" and "society" for historians and for the nature of history as a science or discipline. For me, it was surprising that he, like most German historians up to this time, still emphasized the priority of the term "state" over the term "society" for historians. I was very pleased, however, when he autographed a now rather worn copy of his edition of Hintze's *Staat und Verfassung*.

The year 1967 was also of basic importance for Hintze research since this was the year that Professor Oestreich edited and introduced the third volume of Hintze's *Gesammelte Abhandlungen*—a volume that was titled *Regierung und Verwaltung: Gesammelte Abhandlungen zur Staats- Rechts- und Sozialgeschichte Preussens*.[24] This huge volume (976 pages) was significant for all Hintze research because of the large number of Hintze's writings dealing with Prussian history and also because of Oestreich's introductory

---

23. See Hintze, "Troeltsch and the Problems of Historicism, 377–80; and L. Smith, *Religion and the Rise of History*, 4 and 10.

24. Hintze, *Regierung und Verwaltung*. Hereafter, this volume is cited Hintze, *GA* III. An English translation of this title would be "Government and Administration: Collected Articles on Political-Legal-and Social History of Prussia."

essay called "Otto Hintze und die Verwaltungsgeschichte [Administrative History]." It was also significant for Hintze research because this volume provided both a "Person Register" and a "Subject Register" for all three volumes of this magnificent second edition of Hintze's collected articles. However, since this volume appeared in the same year in which my dissertation was completed, it played no part in the story of the making of my dissertation.

The story behind the making of my dissertation may be of interest not only to Hintze scholars, but also to a general audience because it is a story that is in some ways without parallel in the history of American and European higher education.

During the years from 1964 to 1967, I wrote two dissertations. The first was a complete document that Professor Gerhard said he could accept but that for my sake, it was better that he did not. The second document was one that Professor Gerhard did accept even though it was not finished. After Professor Gerhard had accepted the first chapter of "Otto Hintze's Comparative Constitutional History of the West," I decided not to send each chapter to him one at a time for his approval, but rather to send them together as a whole. One reason for this was because for about half of each year, Professor Gerhard was still in Germany. I soon learned though, that this was not a good idea. When he received and read my whole manuscript, his main objections were that I had many very important things to say that I really didn't develop, and some ideas that were not very important, but which "I drove into the ground." Mainly, Professor Gerhard explained that while I claimed that one of the reasons that Hintze was important was because he incorporated more traditions of nineteenth-century German historiography than any historian of his generation, I had not introduced each of these traditions. What this required was more than a year of additional research, this time using "inter-library loan" books since the closest university research libraries—Iowa, Minnesota, and Wisconsin—were each about 150 miles from Decorah and I didn't have a car.

After this new chapter (which now became chapter two), was complete and approved by Professor Gerhard, the chapters that now became chapters three through seven were reworked and sent to Professor Gerhard. However, before I had finished writing chapter eight (a chapter called "Comparative Constitutional History or Sociology?"), I was astounded when Professor Gerhard informed me that he was retiring from Washington University; that his successor—Professor Theodor H. Von Laue—was already teaching there; and that he had already scheduled my dissertation completion date as early January, 1967 and had arranged a dissertation committee for me because he and his wife were moving to a new permanent residence in Germany.

When I replied that there was no chance that I could finish the last chapter of my dissertation by that date, Professor Gerhard replied that I needed to be in St. Louis the day before this date; that I needed to have five copies of the chapters that were finished; and that I could stay overnight with him. "I am going to take care of you before I leave," he simply said.

The night before I flew from Waterloo, Iowa to St. Louis was the most incredible one of my entire life, for that night I had three typists typing all night long while I was going from one typist to another for them to type in the page numbers. Meanwhile, my wife was making five copies of an unfinished dissertation of more than five hundred pages. Even more incredible, was that, in the chapter where I dealt most of all with material from the Hintze papers in Merseberg, and where Professor Gerhard had indicated in several places where I needed to "check this out," I simply omitted all of these sections. This not only reduced the total number of pages by a considerable amount, but it also led me to devise "the Smith Rule" for my students since that year. That is, both on tests and in papers, "When in doubt, leave it out!"

When I emerged from the administration building with a box-full of dissertation material in order to catch the only flight that could get me to St. Louis on time, I discovered that during the night, all the streets, roads, and highways in and around Decorah were covered with a thin but very treacherous sheet of ice. Thus, for more than twenty miles, I had to drive at a very slow speed with two wheels off of the pavement. When I arrived at this small airport, all of the other passengers were already on the airplane. After running to the plane with a box containing more than 2,500 pages of dissertation material, the pilot held the plane while I purchased a ticket and came running back to the plane. This is what I have always called "a close call." Finally, after I arrived at the Gerhard home, I immediately had to go to the Washington University Library to type and to make five copies of my "Table of Contents."

After all of this, the meeting with my dissertation committee was both something of an anticlimax and a pleasant experience, for no one gave me a hard time. The one requirement that the committee made was that if my dissertation was finished and submitted to the university by the first of May, then I would receive my PhD diploma and hood. The most memorable moment for me, however, was that after the members of the committee had congratulated me, Professor Theodore H. Von Laue privately said to me, "Leonard, stick to this topic, for it could take it you to the top of the profession."

After I had said goodbye to the Gerhards and flew back to Waterloo, I found that my car had a dead battery, for in my haste when I had parked my used, recently purchased, and very inexpensive car,[25] I had neglected to turn off my lights. After I returned to Decorah, I celebrated my success at a big party in our home, and then worked very hard to complete my dissertation. It was a great pleasure for me and my family when I was "hooded" by the Chancellor of Washington University on June 4, 1967.

In December of that year, I attended my first annual meeting of the American Historical Association. At this convention, I was very disappointed in the papers that were presented in the main session that I came to hear, but at the luncheon meeting of the Society for Modern History, I had a very pleasant and interesting encounter with some of the top scholars in this society at this time.

Since I didn't know anyone at this luncheon, I chose one of the remaining chairs at one of the round tables and started reading the name tags: R. R. Palmer, Joel Colton, Crane Brinton, and the name of a third main author of a textbook on European history. I did not recognize the name on the tag that was closest to me, but he was the president of a new branch school of the University of Michigan. When I introduced myself to him as a student of Dietrich Gerhard who had just completed a PhD dissertation on Otto Hintze, his face lit up. "I am a student of Walter Dorn," he said, and then he offered me a job.

During my senior year in college, I had read Dorn's magnificent book on "The "Langer Series," *Competition for Empire 1740–1763* (1940), and from 1958 to 1960, I had used it as a major reference for my courses at Luther College. During my five years of research on Otto Hintze, I learned that Dorn was probably the most knowledgeable, American-born, Hintze scholar of his generation; that this book was dedicated to Otto Hintze (and to Ferdinand Schevill); and that much of what I knew about Prussia and the other "composite" and "Leviathan" states of Europe in 1740 was based both on Dorn and (through the first three chapters of this book), also on

---

25. A 1960 Corvaire, a car that Ralph Nadar made infamous with his book *Unsafe at Any Speed*.

Hintze.[26] In 1945, Dorn used some of his time as an official of the United States military government to track down the lost Hintze manuscripts.

The other interesting part of this story is that when I asked this Dorn student to introduce me to Professor Colton, I asked if he would please inform him that I had used the Palmer/Colton text for many years, and also that I was the professor at Luther College who was most responsible for ordering six-hundred copies of this text each year for all of our first-year students. Professor Palmer was of course, pleased to hear this.

For many years, my dissertation had almost no significance for Hintze research, for it was seldom read or cited. Thus, my emphases on (1) how Hintze did more than any other historian of his generation in Germany to broaden the idea of history as a *Wissenschaft* (science or organized body of knowledge with its own methodology), (2) how Hintze and his friend Meinecke were the two most important historians and connected poles of "the generation of the 1890s" for what H. Stuart Hughes called "The Reorientation of European Thought 1890–1930" in his book called *Consciousness and Society*,[27] and (3) how Hintze and Weber could be seen as the two most important scholars of this generation for the reorientation of European social-historical thought from 1890 to 1933, received no mention or attention for many years. All three of these views were new in 1967; they are still the views that I hold today; and they ran counter both to the views of Gerhard Oestreich in 1967 and the very influential book by Georg G. Iggers, *The German Conception of History: The National Tradition of Historical Thought from Herder to the Present*, which was published in 1968.

Since Oestreich's introductory essay to his addition of Hintze's collected essays in 1964 seemed to indicate that for him Hintze was a pragmatic historian, a political scientist, and a sociologist, I was very interested in Oestreich's article that was published in the *Historische Zeitschrift* in 1969, which focused on the beginning of social-historical research in Germany. In this influential essay, Oestreich showed how (1) at the end of the nineteenth century, both the term and the practice of "social history" were important components of German historiography, (2) how "social history"

---

26. One of the strongest tributes to Hintze in this book is an indirect one: "The final judgment on French administration in the midcentury remains almost as difficult today as it was in the days of de Tocqueville. Until French historians present us with a comprehensive documentary study of every branch of the service comparable to the Prussian *Acta Borussica*, every judgment must remain incomplete and tentative . . ." Dorn, *Competition for Empire 1740–1763*, 34.

27. See Hughes, *Consciousness and Society*.

had been greatly weakened during the great controversy over the work of Karl Lamprecht and "the war against the social scientific wing" of the history profession by many of the most prominent historians in Germany, (3) how Lamprecht, Kurt Breysig, and Otto Hintze were the most prominent and important figures of this "social scientific wing" within the guild of professional historians, (4) how Hintze was not the object of this attack since he was chiefly regarded as a historian of the Prussian state, and (5) how Lamprecht's defeat marked the end of a serious discussion of social history within Germany until after World War II.[28] The main significance of this essay for me, however, was how Oestreich now fully identified himself as a "social historian" and thus departed from the emphasis of his teacher, Hartung, and of his generation of historians who had emphasized political history and the primacy of the state. Thus, Oestreich now was part of that significant turn toward "structural" and "social history" that occurred in Germany in the 1960s.

A very important component of this change within the guild of professional historians in Germany in the 1960s was the influence of American historians who had fled Germany during the 1930s. This influence came not only through the generation of historians who had received their professional training in Germany before they came to the United States, but also through a younger generation who had received their professional training in the United States. In general, it is fair to say that this younger generation of historians was more critical of German historiography as a whole than were their teachers. One of best examples of this is Georg Iggers and his very influential book called *The German Conception of History.*

First of all, this very learned book filled a need, for as Professor Iggers said, "no comprehensive study of German historiography or German historical thought has appeared in English during the past fifty years." This work was not primarily intended as a history of German historiography. Instead, its primary purpose was "to present an interpretative, critical analysis of theoretical presuppositions and political values of the German historians in the major national tradition of German historiography from Wilhelm von Humboldt and Leopold von Ranke to Friedrich Meinecke and Gerhard Ritter."[29] For Iggers, this German conception of history was also referred to as "the classical national tradition of German historicism"[30]—a tradition

28. Oestreich, "Die Fachhistorie," 208.
29. Iggers, *The German Conception of History,* ix.
30. Ibid., xi.

that "continued to be closely interwoven with a *Weltanschauung* and a set of values that remained relatively static in the face of changing intellectual and social conditions."[31] "In this book," Iggers also explained, "when we speak of historicism, we shall generally refer to the main tradition of German historiography and historical thought which has dominated historical writing, the cultural sciences, and political theory in Germany from Wilhelm von Humboldt and Leopold von Ranke until the recent past."[32]

From the time this book was printed, I had a number of problems with it. First of all, when Iggers stated that his study "consciously violated the spirit of German historicism, for it not only seeks to understand but to judge,"[33] this ran counter both to my experience as a soldier in Germany from 1955–56 and my experience as a student of Dietrich Gerhard. When I arrived in Germany toward the end of "the U.S. occupation," I was both very curious and quite judgmental concerning German history as a whole. One of the first and main lessons that I learned at this time, however, was that nothing gets in the way of understanding more than judging. This basic view was reinforced for me later by Professor Gerhard, for any time I sought to emphasize how my views were important and unique by criticizing the views of others, he would say, "cut out the polemics, for your purpose is not to judge but to persuade."

Secondly, my views (1) that Hintze could be seen as a central figure for German historiography from 1890 to 1933 because he combined and advanced more traditions of nineteenth-century historiography than any professional historians of this generation, and (2) that Hintze and Meinecke could be seen as the two most important and connected poles for understanding the nature and significance of German and Western historical thought at that time, were very different than the view that Iggers presented. For Iggers, it was no coincidence that Friedrich Meinecke was the one historian who was cited only slightly fewer times than Ranke in the index for this book, for to a considerable degree, this book rests on Meinecke's view that historicism was basically a *Weltanschauung* that was based on an "individualizing observation" or way of viewing life.[34]

While Iggers was one of the first American historians to discuss the importance of Otto Hintze for modern German historiography, here

---

31. Ibid., ix–x.
32. Ibid., 4.
33. Ibid., 13.
34. Meinecke, *Historism*, iv.

he was seen not as a part of the "main tradition," but rather as a scholar whose thought and work represented "a challenge to traditional historical concepts."[35] Although my name and my dissertation were not mentioned in this book, in 1970 Professor Iggers did ask me for corrections and suggestions for the German addition of this book, which I was pleased to do.

The single most important contribution to Hintze studies in the United States and to the entire English-speaking world appeared in the year 1975 when Oxford University Press published *The Historical Essays of Otto Hintze: Edited with an Introduction by Felix Gilbert*. As Gilbert said in the preface of this work, "Clearly it was not possible to publish more than a selection from the three large volumes of *Otto Hintze: Gesammelte Abhandlungen*," and the first main principle behind the selection process was to translate essays from each of the three main areas with which Hintze was concerned—Prussian history, comparative history, and historical theory. In addition, the essays within each section were presented chronologically so that they represented the main periods of Hintze's work.[36] In this preface, Gilbert also emphasized the great difficulty he had in translating these essays and how this task proved to be much greater than he had originally imagined.[37]

When Professor Gerhard had informed me both about this project and its contents, I wrote to Professor Gilbert and suggested that if this book included Hintze's three ideal types—feudalism, estates structures (*ständische Verfassungen*), and the modern state—it would be more useful for me and other history teachers to use since together they represented a complete typology of Western institutional development. In reply, Professor Gilbert politely informed me why this desirable goal could not be accomplished in this volume.

As a teacher in a "World Civilizations" course, however, I strongly believed (and still believe) that a small book containing these three essays could be very useful for college and university history teachers who teach classes in "Western Civilization" or "World Civilizations." Therefore, I contacted Professor Leonard Krieger at the University of Chicago to see if he would be interested in adding a book about Otto Hintze to the excellent series of books on great historians that he edited. Such a book would mainly consist of a translation of Hintze's three ideal types.

---

35. Iggers, *The German Conception of History*, 232.
36. Gilbert, "Preface" to *The Historical Essays of Otto Hintze*, v.
37. Ibid., vi.

At first, Krieger was very attracted to this idea. However, after he had proposed this idea to his publishers, they firmly rejected the idea after learning about the financial loss Oxford University Press had experienced in publishing *The Historical Essays of Otto Hintze*. The reason that this little story is significant is (1) that in a letter to Gerhard Oestreich, I had informed him of my hopes to translate these three essays under the title "Otto Hintze's Historical Typology of the West," and (2) that in an extensive essay that began and ended with reference to the Gilbert book of Hintze's essays, Oestreich reported that "hopefully" this work would "soon be supplemented" by a book by Leonard S. Smith under the title mentioned above.[38] Thus, the first important reference to me and to my dissertation in German literature was to a project that I was dreaming about and that probably was too difficult for me "to handle."

The most important conclusion that I drew from Krieger's letter was that if historians, history teachers, and college and university libraries in the United States would not purchase a work on Hintze that was as significant as this book of essays and that had an editor as well-known and respected as Felix Gilbert, then what publisher would take a chance on publishing a work on this topic by a totally unknown historian? Therefore, I decided that I had to make myself and my topic known to the history profession in some other way.

Since by the year 1980, I had created a typology of Western historical thought that was based on Hintze's ideal-type methodology in a year-long, interdisciplinary (English, History, Philosophy, and Religion), and had devised a great-books honors seminar for college freshman, I decided to present this news as a part of a session that I organized for the annual meeting of the American Historical Association that was held in Los Angeles, California on December 28–30, 1981. Both the titles of the papers and most of the names of the participants in this session (titled "The German Universities and Historical Thought"), were impressive. Peter Hanns Reill was the chair of the session; Georg G. Iggers presented a paper titled "The University of Göttingen and the Transformation of Historical Studies, 1760–1800"; Rudolf Vierhaus presented a paper titled "The German Universities and the Historical Sciences in the Nineteenth Century"[39]; and the

---

38. Oestreich, "Otto Hintze: Tradition und Fortschrift," 127.

39. Vierhaus was not able to present his paper in person, and he was the one who recommended that Rüsen appear on the program in his place. Peter Celms was the other commentator on the three papers.

title of my paper was "Otto Hintze and a Historical Typology of Western Historiography." The names Reill, Iggers, and especially Vierhaus, who was the Director of the Max-Planck Institüt für Geschichte, were well known to all scholars in the field of German history, and Jörn Rüsen, one of the two commentators, was relatively unknown at the time, but later became a well-known historian in the field of German historiography. The title of my paper was never published and only became important much later when this typology became a framework for a book that eventually became *Religion and the Rise of History: Martin Luther and the Cultural Revolution in Germany 1760–1810* (2009).

The year 1980 was a major year for Hintze research and studies, since from April 24 to 26 of that year, a conference called "Otto Hintze und die Moderne Geschichtswissenschaft" was held in Berlin. The two main speakers and honorary guests for this international conference that included 64 participants were two Meinecke students who had known Otto Hintze, Dietrich Gerhard, and Felix Gilbert. Before Gerhard presented the opening address at this conference, he had already published the best essay in English on the nature and significance of Otto Hintze in an article in 1970.[40] Gerhard's excellent opening address, called "Otto Hintze: Personality and Work," was and still is a very important contribution to Hintze research and literature for many reasons. One important reason is that Gerhard provided valuable new information based on his own conversations not only with Otto Hintze, but also with Hedwig Hintze.

While the main point of Gilbert's address was that while historians in Germany identified more with Hintze than with any historian of his time, he was more of a "forerunner" than "a founder" of "*Die modern Geschichtswissenschaft.*" For me, the most useful aspect of this thoughtful and very inclusive essay was that for Hintze "History is *Wissenschaft* and nothing but *Wissenschaft,*" for there was no trace of rhetoric in his work.[41]

The fact that this volume contained many valuable essays on all aspects of Hintze's work; that they were written by many of the leading historians in Germany at that time; and that together they provide the best bibliographical source for all the literature concerning Otto Hintze to that time, make the volume *Otto Hintze und die Moderne Geschichtswissenschaft: Eine*

---

40. Gerhard, "Otto Hintze: His Work and Significance in Historiography."
41. Gilbert, "Otto Hintze und die moderne Geschichtswissenschaft." 206.

Tagungsbericht,[42] which was published in 1983, a high point of literature on Hintze to the present.

Although I was invited to be a participant in this international conference, and although my transportation costs were paid for by the *Historische Kommission zu Berlin*, my chief contribution was to hold up a light-brown "t-shirt"—at Professor Gerhard's suggestion—that my students and colleagues had presented to me at California Lutheran College on the morning that I flew from Los Angeles, California to Berlin, with an inscription in large black letters: "*Otto Hintze is Number 1.*"[43] A second contribution was my statement that for me, Hintze's ideal type of the modern state was the most useful of his three famous models. However, when I added that my main teaching course was called "World Civilizations," there were chuckles all around. What the directors of this conference appreciated most of all from me, however, was a copy of my microfilm reel of documents from the Hintze papers in Merseburg. Also, since Gerhard Oestreich had died in 1978, I was probably the only participant at this conference who had done research in the Hintze papers that were still located in Merseburg.

Two of the highlights of this conference for me were the opportunities to interview both Gerhard and Gilbert in their apartments in that wonderful complex of the *Historischer Kommission zu Berlin*. Before I interviewed Professor Gerhard, I had read and copied two letters in the Meinecke papers that he had written to Meinecke—one at the outbreak of World War I and the other, a description of what it was like teaching history in the United States, which was written shortly after World War II. Both of these letters are ones that should be translated and published. However, my interest at this time was to have Dr. Gerhard read the first of these letters to me, to his wife, and to my tape recorder, for the letter was a beautiful statement of how Meinecke's first great intellectual history had led him to want to become a professional historian, and how overcome he was with emotion at the outbreak of that turning point in history that is now called World War I.

My interview with Gilbert was also memorable, first of all because he emphasized that if he had known how difficult it would prove to be to

---

42. Büsch and Erbe, eds. *Otto Hintze und die Moderne Geschichtswissenschaft.*

43. It was extraordinarily fortunate for me that my first and main undergraduate history teacher, Dr. Irvine Dowie, was a "Senior Mentor" for the History Department at California Lutheran University at this time. He offered to teach all of my classes not only for this week, but also for a second week so that I could do more research in Berlin. Dr. Dowie was the only historian I have ever known who earned a PhD when he was blind, and he was one of the kindest professional historians that I have ever known.

translate *The Historical Essays of Otto Hintze*, he might not have undertaken this project. Secondly, when I remarked how interesting it was that it was two Meinecke students who had done more to promote Hintze studies in the United States than anyone else, he informed me that the main influence of Meinecke students for American historiography was in the field of Renaissance studies. Indeed, when scholars in this field met, it was something of a reunion of Meinecke students.

In the year 1993, Wolfgang Neugebauer made a very significant contribution to Hintze literature and studies in an article called "Otto Hintze und seine Konzeption der 'Allgemeinen Verfassungsgeschichte der neueren Staaten.'" This was significant because Neugebauer not only had made an intensive study of the material in the Hintze Nachlass that was now available in an undivided Berlin,[44] but also because he had acquired a previously unknown four-hundred page student manuscript from Hintze's lecture course in the winter semester 1910/11 called "Allgemeine Verfassungsgeschichte der neueren Staaten." Through this material, as well as through the student manuscript with this title, which Professor Oestreich had allowed me to see in 1964, Neugebauer thought it was no longer possible to say that Hintze's "General Constitutional History of the Modern States" no longer existed.[45] Additionally, Neugebauer claimed that since this lecture contained the chapters that were missing in the Hintze papers and that were supposedly lost, one could now say that Hintze's main life work still existed.[46]

With this essay, the literature concerning Otto Hintze's first main goal of his life—the creation of "a general comparative constitutional history and administrative history of the states of the modern world, particularly of Latin and Germanic nations" had to be revised. It especially had to be revised in light of the statement about Hintze's lecture courses in his

---

44. Neugebauer, "Otto Hintze und seine Konzeption," 68. Neugebauer was first able to see these papers, he said, in 1989 and 1991.

45. Ibid., 68. The new manuscript which Neugebauer had discovered was cited "Titelblatt Berlin W. S. 1910/11. Professor Dr, Hintze. Allgemeine Verfassungsgeschichte der neuren Staaten. Otto Gloeden," p. 88, while later references are cited "Ms *Gloeden*." The reference that Neugebauer uses for the lecture that Oestreich allowed me to see in 1964, is cited by Neugebauer as: Generallandsarchiv Karlsruh, Nachlass Krebs 37, Mitschrift aus den Winter Semester 1913/14: Otto Hintze, "Verfassungsgeschichte der neueran Staaten." Ibid., 86, n. 94. Hereafter Neugebauer cites this manuscript as "Ms *Krebs*. In addition to these manuscripts see other manuscripts listed in this note (n. 96), and n. 88 on p. 88.

46. Ibid., 90.

"Entrance Address" after he had stated that Prussia would be a paradigm for him.

"So I have been concerned with the institutions of Austria, Spain, the Netherlands, Switzerland, individual Italian states, above all France, England, the Americas, also the Scandinavian lands, Hungary, Poland, and Russia and other exotic states, at least as far as this is possible without a knowledge of their language. Out of these studies I gradually, and next in a special lecture which handled the most important states, built up my larger lecture over the constitutional history of the modern nations [*neuere Völker*], which was the chief object of my university teaching activity and which in the foreseeable future I hoped to publish in a book."[47]

Using this key from Hintze's "Entrance Address" to the Royal Prussian Academy of Sciences" in 1914, the lecture notes cited above, and the material on Hintze papers, Neugebauer then formulated a new conception of Hintze's "Allgemeinen Verfassungsgeschichte der neuren Staaten." Since the one previous conception of Hintze's chief goal was my dissertation called "Otto Hintze's Comparative Constitutional History of the West," my dissertation now—for the first time—became a matter of real significance for the literature dealing with the work of Otto Hintze. The best indications of this were (1) that it was the only work cited in the notes that was preceeded by the word "important," (2) that this was the first work by a German scholar to cite this dissertation extensively, and (3) that it was cited seventeen times.

This essay was followed five years later (1998) with the publication of Otto Hintze's, *Allgemeine Verfassungs- und Verwaltungsgeschichte der neueren Staaten: Fragmente Band I,* which was edited by Giuseppe Di Constanzo, Michael Erbe, and Wolfgang Neugebauer and published by Palomar. Here, almost all of the material in the Hintze papers that had not previously been published was now in print. While Part I included Scandinavia, Denmark, Sweden, Poland in the Middle Ages, Hungary, and the Netherlands, Part II included Switzerland, Austria, Italy (with sections on Upper Italy, Savoy-Piedmont, Venice, Florence, Rome, Sardinia, and Sicily), and Spain.

In addition, this volume contained a Forward by the editors; a "Presentazione" by Fulvio Tessitore; an "Introduzione" by Giuseppe Di Costanzo; and Wolfgang Neugebauer's essay, "Otto Hintze und Seine Konzeption der 'Allgemeinen Verfassungsgeschichte der neueren Staaten"—an essay that was an expansion of the article that was first published in 1993. Here again, my dissertation was cited with the word "important," but in this expanded

---

47. Hintze, "Antrittsrede," 564–65.

essay, my dissertation was cited 20 times. With this book, my basic conception of what Hintze's comparative constitutional history would have been like had it ever been published had now been superseded. What this book did not explain, however, is what happened to Hintze's lecture called *Politik* or *Allgemeine Staatslehre*.

In the year 2004, another major contribution to the literature on Otto Hintze was published: Otto Hintze and Hedwig Hintze, "*Versage nicht und lass nicht ab zu kämpfen . . .": Die Korrespondence 1925–1940*, which was compiled by Britta Oestreich and edited by Robert Jütte and Gerhard Hirschfeld (Esssen: Klartext Verlag, 2004).[48] In her Introduction to this book, Brigitta Oestreich provided an important supplement to her essay in the year 1985, called "Hedwig und Otto Hintze. Eine biographische Skizze," in *Geschichte und Gesellschaft*—a book in which the date of Hedwig Hintze's death was first established and in which I was credited as the person who first established this date.[49]

In this book, "*Versage nicht und lass nicht ab zu kämpfen . . .*," part of a letter from me dated November 9, 1978 concerning the information that I was able to ascertain about Hedwig Hintze's death in Utrecht was included, and she translated it for the book. What I reported to her was that the police there could give me no information, but the bureau for *Bevölkerungsregister* had provided me with the date of her death: 19 July 1942. I also reported that the last address that I could find for her was the Akademische Krankenhaus Utrecht and that the only document that this hospital still possessed was an admittance card with her name, date of birth, and the handwritten diagnosis of "Endogene Depression." Since part of the building where the hospital records were kept had been destroyed by bombing attacks in October or November of the year 1944, that seemed to be all the information that I could ascertain at this time. The hospital, I added, had no information about what happened with her body and didn't know anything about a suicide. In conclusion, I said that at least I had been able to establish the date of her death.

This letter to Brigitta Oestreich was important not only because I had established the date of Hedwig Hintze's death and the kind of depression

---

48. A literal translation of the main part of this title is: "Don't Deny and Don't Cease to Fight."

49. B. Oestreich, "Hedwig und Otto Hintze," 418. Unfortunately, Brigitta Oestreich added something that was not in my letter when she said that the cause of Hedwig Hintze's death was "endogene depression," for my only information from this hospital was from an admittance card.

that she was suffering when she was admitted to the hospital, but also because I could not find any information in this short visit to Utrecht about a possible suicide. This was important because in my dissertation, I had stated what the Oestreich's and others assumed: that "Hedwig Hintze died by her own hand in Holland when that country was controlled by Hitler and the National Socialists."[50] It was very unfortunate that both in the Foreword and in Brigitta Ostreich's "Introduction," however, Hedwig Hintze's "suicide" was emphasized as a fact at the very time when Peter Th. Walther had discovered that she had not committed suicide. Thus, today we know much more about the final days of Hedwig Hintze especially through Walther's work.[51]

In April 2009, my decades-long study called *Religion and the Rise of History: Martin Luther and the Cultural Revolution in Germany 1760–1810* (Eugene, Oregon: Cascade Books) was published. Although Hintze's name was not mentioned in the title, from beginning to end it dealt with the significance of Otto Hintze for Western historical thought. It did this first of all because this intellectual history was "the first study to apply the ideal-type methodology of Otto Hintze (1861–1940) to Western historical thought as a whole, or to what R. G. Collingwood called 'The Idea of History,' for it contains succinct and useful models for seeing and teaching (1) the classical historiography of Greece and Rome, (2) Christian historiography from the time of St. Augustine to Voltaire, and (3) a distinctly modern type of Western historiography."[52] While the last chapter dealt with modern professional historiography from Leopold von Ranke (1795–1886) to Otto Hintze and was called "From a Holy Hieroglyph to a *Wissenschaft* Alone: History as a Calling and Profession from Ranke to Hintze," the last part of this chapter was called "Ranke and Demystifying the Rankean View of History." Here, I summarized the two main views that I had stressed in the two last chapters of my dissertation: (1) the significance of the three-way discussion between Ernst Troeltsch (1865–1923), Friedrich Meinecke, and Hintze concerning the nature of "historicism" for the reorientation of Western historical thought from 1890 to 1936, and (2) the significance of Hintze and Max Weber as the two poles of European social-historical

---

50. Smith, "Otto Hintze's Comparative Constitutional History of the West," 85. For the Oestreich's assumption that Hedwig Hintze died by her own hand in a "Nervenklinik," see the reference to a letter from Erich Kaufman to G. Oestreich on 13. 4. 1964 in B. Oestreich, "Hedwig und Otto Hintze," 418.

51. Smith, *Religion and the Rise of History*, 231–32.

52. Ibid., ix.

thought within that generation of scholars which H. Stuart Hughes called "the generation of the 1890s" in his ground-breaking work *Consciousness and Society: The Reorientation of European Thought 1890–1930* (1958).

Since these ideas were embedded in a book that focused on two other original, large, and significant ideas, I believed that I had finally placed Hintze in a context that American scholars could not ignore. "*Religion and the Rise of History*," I emphasized, "is the first work to suggest that in addition to his well-known paradoxical, *simul*, and/or 'at-the-same time' way of thinking and viewing life, Martin Luther also had had a deeply incarnational, dynamic, and/or 'in-with-and-under way.'" This dual vision, I also emphasized, "strongly influenced Leibniz, Hamann, Herder, and Ranke "and was therefore a matter of considerable significance for what Friedrich Meinecke (1862–1954) called "the rise of historicism."[53]

The third major idea in this book, I claimed, was that "this essay suggests a new way of seeing, dating, and naming the formative stage of modern German thought, culture, and education"—a period that I called *The Cultural Revolution in Germany, 1760–1810*, and "a period that began in the early 1760s and culminated with the founding of the University of Berlin, the first fully 'modern' and 'modernizing' university, and the Prussian and German *Gymnasium*."[54]

Today, it is possible that this study has provided some assistance in reaching the two main goals of my academic life: (1) to make Hintze's thought and work more accessible to the English-speaking world, and (2) to show how he was and still remains what Meinecke first claimed—one of the great ones in the discipline. The best indication that this book could be an important step in the realization of these two goals can be found in the concluding words of a review of *Religion and the Rise of History* that appeared in *The American Historical Review* in October 2011, for here, Richard L. Gawthrop wrote: "Nevertheless, *Religion and the Rise of History*, the product of several decades of teaching, reading, and reflection, is a work of outstanding originality and deserves a wide readership. Smith's thesis has major, potentially transformative, implications for the fields of historiography, German cultural history, and the history of Western Christianity."[55]

---

53. Ibid., Meinecke, *Die Entstehung der Historismus*.
54. Ibid.
55. Gawthrop, Review of *Religion and the Rise of History*, by Leonard S. Smith. 1211–12.

The Expert's Historian

In the fall semester 2009, my wife and I visited several Lutheran colleges in Iowa and Minnesota and a Lutheran seminary to publicize *Religion and the Rise of History*. For this trip, I decided that the most helpful thing that I could do both to publicize this book and to promote the significance of Otto Hintze to history teachers and students was to combine my three ideal types of Western historiography from my book with the classroom presentation that I had given for many years that I called "Historicism as a Method of Teaching Students How To Write a History Paper."

If I presented these models together on a two-sided handout; if I selected three representative quotations from each of the three main periods of Western historiography (also on a two-sided handout); and if I could go through these quotations in twenty-five minutes so that I would still have time to present my "Historicism as a Method" presentation, I thought this would be something that no other historian in the world could do or would even consider doing.

Thus, for the first time, such a presentation was given twice in a "World Civilizations" discussion period at California Lutheran University, once in a history class at Luther College, and once at St. Olaf College. In each case, the kind instructor who allowed me to do this presentation had never heard of the ideas stemming from Hintze that modern historical thought is basically analogical; that it is based on the modern concepts of "individuality" and "development"; and that these two concepts are based on the analogy of a "unit of life" or a person *and* on the analogy of a "process of life" or the life of a single human being.

Whether the instructors in each case accepted this very different way of teaching history and the idea of history, each time at least some of the students were able to see "the idea of history" and to see the value of Hintze's understanding of historicism as a method for writing a paper that could be called a *history* paper. Most of all, however, each student had what no other students in the world possessed: a two-sided copy of my typology of Western historiography from the book *Religion and the Rise of History* and a two-sided sheet of quotations for understanding the idea of history from Herodotus to Hintze.

My final fifty-year encounter with the significance of what Troeltsch, Meinecke, and Hintze called "historicism" for understanding Western historical thought as a whole happened in 2012, when I learned that Frederick C. Beiser had just published a book called *The German Historicist Tradition* (2011). I had admired, used, and frequently cited Beiser's books—*The*

Fate of Reason (1987) and *Enlightenment, Revolution, and Romanticism* (1992)—as well as his article, "Hegel's Historicism" from *The Cambridge Companion to Hegel* (1993), within my study called *Religion and the Rise of History*. As such, I was very eager to learn who Beiser included in his latest book.

First of all, I knew that in the second of these three studies, Beiser accepted, used, and broadened Meinecke's definition of historicism[56] as a basic term for understanding German philosophy. Secondly, I guessed that this book would probably cover German thought from the late eighteenth century through the time and work of Friedrich Meinecke—an assumption that proved to be correct.

The German Historicist Tradition, Beiser stated, "is a re-examination of 'the old historicism', the classical historicist tradition that began in Germany with Claudenius in the middle of the eighteenth century and that ended with Max Weber at the beginning of the twentieth century."[57] His chief task, he said, was to "introduce the Anglophone reader to the major figures in the historicist tradition." While "The main precedent and model for this work has been Friedrich Meinecke's *Entstehung des Historismus*," his approach, he added, was both historical and systematic.[58]

In his "Introduction: The Concept and Context of Historicism," Beiser began his first section—"An intellectual revolution"—with this sentence: "In 1936, in the nostalgic preface to his magisterial *Die Enstehung des Historismus*, Friederick Meinecke wrote that historicism was 'one of the greatest revolutions experienced by Western thought.'"[59] In his helpful discussion of the way Meinecke and others have defined the term "historicism," Beiser chose to define historicism "by determining the common characteristics of those who contributed to it."[60] Using this as a guideline, he said he would define historicism "along the lines of Ernst Troeltsch, who first introduced the word in its modern sense, which meant "the fundamental historization of all our thinking about man, his culture, and his values."[61] For Beiser, "Besides its central theme of the omnipresence of historical change, there are

---

56. Beiser, *Enlightenment, Revolution, and Romanticism*, 5–6.
57. Ibid.
58. Ibid.
59. Ibid., 1.
60. Ibid., 2.
61. Ibid.

two further defining principles of historicism." While the first of these was "the principle of individuality," the "second defining principle is holism."[62]

Although from beginning to end, *The German Historicist Tradition* is an encounter with both Meinecke and Troeltsch, neither of them were dealt with as separate subjects. This is especially surprising since Beiser did include Georg Simmel (1858–1918) and ended with Max Weber. Most surprising of all, however, is that Beiser did not include Otto Hintze, the best philosophically trained mind of all the professional historians of this age in Germany and the one who probed most deeply into the philosophical problems of the day. It is also especially surprising since for Beiser, "the concept of historicism developed here . . . makes an historicist anyone who contributed substantially to the program of justifying the scientific status of history."[63]

It was my encounter with Beiser's magisterial work, *The German Historicist Tradition*, however, that inspired me to write this book. From the time that my dissertation was completed in 1967, I had planned—and frequently worked on—a vastly reduced (less than 300 pages) and updated version of my dissertation, but with a completely different title. During the 1980s and early 1990s, I did update chapter two of my dissertation by dividing it into six smaller chapters, each dealing with a main tradition of nineteenth-century German historiography that was helpful for understanding Hintze's work. Unfortunately, at this time, however, I was still using WordPerfect rather than Word and still using endnotes rather than footnotes.

Fortunately, however, with my introductions to the work of Ranke, Droysen, Schmoller, Dilthey, Hintze, Meinecke, and Troeltsch in my dissertation (1967), with my *Religion and the Rise of History* (2009), with Beiser's masterful treatment of the first four of these scholars in *The German Historicist Tradition* (2011), and with the present study (2013), every "Anglophone reader" will have a sufficient base to begin the study of Otto Hintze's significance for the idea of history and the German historicist tradition. To encourage all historians and philosophers to read this book by Beiser, and to show Hintze's significance for the German historicist tradition, however, chapter four of this book is a critical review of Beiser's *The German Historicist Tradition*.

For more than two thousand years of Western historical thought, history was commonly regarded as an art that was based on teaching

---

62. Ibid., 4.
63. Ibid., 9.

philosophy by example. Today, I close my fifty-year encounter with the work of Otto Hintze with a classroom presentation. It is called "Teaching the Idea of History and Historicism as a Method for Writing a History Paper." It consists of the three ideal types that provided the structure for my book *Religion and the Rise of History*; three selected quotations from each of the three main periods of Western historical thought to illustrate each part of this story; and my use of Hintze's definition of historicism in assigning a paper in a World Civilizations course and informing my students how I would grade their papers. Thus, this epilogue can be seen as the culmination of my fifty-year quest: "to make it easier for the world to approach his work."

In the endorsement on the back cover to *Religion and the Rise of History*, Thomas a Brady Jr. wrote: "Leonard Smith's book is, in its origins and goals, a deeply pedagogical work." Like this study, *The Expert's Historian: Otto Hintze and the Nature of Modern Historical Thought*," is a deeply pedagogical work. It is also a very American work, for from beginning to end, it is based not only on Hintze's understanding of the term "historicism," but also on that very American ideal best captured in the immortal words of Clint Eastwood, "It works for me."

2

Meinecke, Troeltsch, Hintze, and the Discovery of Historicism as a Methodology

IN THE YEAR 1941, Friedrich Meinecke (1862–1954) called his friend Otto Hintze "one of the great ones in the discipline." In the year 1947, Felix Gilbert wrote an article for *The American Historical Review* wherein he said, "There is no doubt that with the perspective which only the passage of time provides, Hintze emerges as the most important figure in German historical scholarship of the twentieth century . . ."[1] One of the most interesting aspects of this quotation is that it was written by a student of Friedrich Meinecke, the most famous and influential German historian of the twentieth century, seven years before Meinecke's death.

In the year 1967, I completed a dissertation called "Otto Hintze's Comparative Constitutional History of the West"—a 617-page study that is still the most detailed and fully documented account of Hintze's training, publications, and career. Today, this dissertation is available through interlibrary loan, but only from Germany, which is a good indication of how much it has influenced the education of history students in the United States. To partially rectify this situation, I have given copies of this dissertation to the libraries of California Lutheran University, Washington University in St.

---

1. Gilbert, "German Historiography during the Second World War," 52–53; and Smith, "Otto Hintze's Comparative Constitutional History of the West," 88.

Louis, and the University of California Los Angeles, which have given me full and free access since 1969.

The two main purposes behind this dissertation and all of my work since the year 1967, have been to show how Hintze became "one of the great ones in the discipline" and how he "emerges as the most important figure in German historical scholarship of the twentieth century." These are still the main goals behind this essay, and today I have some suggestions as to what future historians in the English-speaking or "the Anglophone world," can learn from him.

To be recognized as one of the great ones in the discipline called history, a great historian is usually included in historiography courses in major universities and colleges. Today, most major research libraries probably have copies of the three volumes of *Otto Hintze Gesammelte Abhandlungen*, which were edited by Gerhard Oestreich. Many smaller universities and colleges in the United States that offer courses in historiography however, do not have all three of these volumes, nor do they have sufficiently-translated Hintze articles and secondary sources in English for their students to study in order to write a competent research paper on Hintze and his work.

What would they need most of all? Most of all they would need to have access to *The Historical Essays of Otto Hintze* that was edited by Felix Gilbert in 1975, for it contains eleven important English translations from the three main areas of Hintze's research and publications: Prussian History, Comparative and Administrative History, and History and Theory. Of these eleven articles, the article "Troeltsch and the Problems of Historicism: Critical Studies" is the one that should be of interest to all historians, for it contains Hintze's brilliant but often ignored, definition of historicism as a method for doing history. This was one of the main points of my dissertation in 1967; of the last chapter of my book *Religion and the Rise of History* in 2009; and the main point and idea of the "Epilogue: Teaching the Idea of History and Historicism as a Method for Writing a History Paper" in the present study.

Although the name Otto Hintze does not appear in the title of *Religion and the Rise of History*, one of its main purposes was to introduce him, his work as a whole, and the Troeltsch article to the "Anglophone reader," to the "Anglophone world," and to an "Anglophone audience."[2] Here, the context for this introduction to Hintze's work was much broader than in

---

2. For these terms, I am indebted to Frederick C. Beiser and his "Preface" to *The German Historicist Tradition*, vii.

my dissertation, for here, Hintze's work was placed in the whole context of Western historiography from the time of Herodotus and/or to what R. G. Collingwood called *The Idea of History*.

The main way I did this was through a historical typology of Western historiography as a whole, for it contained "succinct and useful models for seeing, understanding, and teaching (1) the classical historiography of Greece and Rome, (2) Christian historiography from the time of St. Augustine to Voltaire, and (3) a distinctly modern type of Western historiography."[3] Even though Hintze's name does not appear in the title of this book, from beginning to end it was based on Hintze's ideal-type or model-building methodology and his significance for the idea of history as a whole.

While this study is also a book that every college or university that offers a course in historiography should have, the most extensive and detailed secondary source in the English language for a knowledge of Hintze's training, writings, and career is still my unpublished dissertation, "Otto Hintze's Comparative Constitutional History of the West" (1967). Although it was not the first dissertation on Hintze either in Germany or in the United States, it was the first to be based on two full years of research in Germany (1962–64), on three years of additional research and writing while teaching in the United States (1964–67), on archival research both in Berlin and Merseburg (1964), and on all of Hintze's published writings, including 248 book reviews.

One of the reasons this dissertation is still useful today is because it was written before almost any of Hintze's articles had been translated into English.[4] Therefore, I believed that I had to include summaries of almost everything he had written for the Anglophone reader. While on the one-hand, this contributed to the unusual length of this dissertation, it also meant that for understanding Hintze's work as a whole, it is still an especially good secondary source for Anglophone readers.

For all readers, however, this dissertation is still important for the ways I viewed the significance of Hintze's work both for German and Western historical thought. First of all, he continued, broadened, and advanced more traditions of nineteenth-century German historiography than any

---

3. Smith, *Religion and the Rise of History*, ix.

4. For the first Hintze essay to be translated into English, see Smith, "Otto Hintze's Comparative Constitutional History of the West," 77–79. See here how this particular Hintze essay, its title, and it origins were distinctive. Henceforth, page references to my 1967 study will be listed in parentheses in the text.

historian of his generation. Most of all, he successfully supplemented and broadened Leopold von Ranke's tradition called "The Latin and Germanic Nations," for from the beginning, he focused on that community of nations which grew out of the Latin Christendom. As Dietrich Gerhard pointed out, as far as he knew, Hintze was the only researcher who throughout his entire life, was occupied with the distinctiveness of the constitutional structure of the Occidental European states.[5]

Second, just as from the beginning, Ranke was interested in showing how the Latin and Germanic nations as a whole were distinctive in the context of universal or world history, so from the beginning one can see how all of Hintze's work aimed to show how Latin Christendom or the West was distinctive in comparison with other civilizations (37–39). While Ranke had concentrated primarily on the interaction of modern European states and great political events, Hintze chose to supplement Ranke's work by concentrating on the internal structures of the Western states.

One of the least known, but most important, stories contained in my dissertation is how among the scholars of the generation of the 1890's, "Otto Hintze continued the intellectual heritage of Dilthey in the most creative way" (172). The term, "the generation of the 1890's" was a term that I borrowed from H. Stuart Hughes and his classic intellectual history, *Consciousness and Society: The Reorientation of European Social Thought 1890–1930*. For Hughes, this was a generation which came of age intellectually around the year 1890 and whose birthdates fell between 1856 and 1877 (16). One of the great strengths of my dissertation as a whole was that it placed the work of Otto Hintze in the context provided by this book even though Hintze was never mentioned. It was also the main context that I used in 2009 for the second half of the last chapter—a chapter that focused on the significance of Otto Hintze for the reorientation of modern Western social-historical thought in the first third of the twentieth century.

In the year 1882, Wilhelm Dilthey became a professor of philosophy at the University of Berlin, and in 1883, he published his most influential work, *Einleitung in die Geisteswissenschaften* or *Introduction to the Human Sciences*. One of the reasons that this work was so influential was because by the last years of the nineteenth century, it was common to speak of the natural sciences, but there was no generally accepted name for those academic disciplines that were not natural sciences. Thus, when Dilthey suggested that the sciences could be divided into two main branches—into

---

5. Gerhard, "Otto Hintze: Persönlichkeit und Werk," 13.

the natural sciences and the *Geisteswissenschaften*—this was not only one of the milestones on the road to the separation and division of sciences and the unity of the scholarly world (139), but it was also a matter of importance for all academic sciences or disciplines.

In this study, Dilthey attempted to provide a theory of knowledge not only for history, but also for all of the sciences that were concerned with "historical-social reality," for as the subtitle of this work proclaimed, it was "An Attempt to Establish a Foundation for the Study of Society and History."[6] In my dissertation in 1967, I translated and summarized not only some of the main ideas of this book in a section called "Dilthey and the Problems of the Natural Sciences, The Human Studies, and History" (138–72), but also some of the main ideas of his two greatest critics, Wilhelm Windelband and Heinrich Rickert, plus Karl Menger and the launching of a "methodological controversy" with Gustav Schmoller in the year 1883 (158–62).[7] Today, these pages are still a useful introduction to these scholars, especially in relation to Hintze's work and his definition and discussion of "historicism" in the essay "Troeltsch and the Problems of Historicism."[8]

In 1880, after two years of study at the University of Greifswald, where he was listed as a student of philology and where he also studied history and philosophy, Otto Hintze registered as a student at the University of Berlin. Here, he was drawn, most of all, to the study of history and to the historian Johann Gustav Droysen. Hintze was a member of the inner circle of students surrounding Droysen and served as the last librarian of Droysen's "Historical Society," the forerunner of the Historical Seminar at the University of Berlin (4). Since Dilthey became a professor at Berlin in 1882 and Droysen died in 1884, the only time when Hintze could have been trained by the two greatest scholars of their day for the theory of history was from 1882 to 1884.[9] As members of Hintze's dissertation commit-

---

6. Dilthey, *Einleitung in die Geistewissneschaften*. This is volume 1 of *Wilhelm Dilthey's Gesammelte Schriften*. Unfortunately, this subtitle does not appear on the title page of the English edition of Dilthey's *Introduction to the Human Sciences*, vol. 1 of *Selected Works*, edited by Rudolf A. Makkreel and Frithjof Rodi.

7. For a brief, excellent, and recent summary of the nature and significance of the *Methodenstreit*, the "dispute between Carl Menger (1840–1921), the head of the Austrian school of economics and Gustav Schmoller (1838–1917), the leader of the so-called 'younger historical school'" about the proper method for economics, especially for Max Weber, see Beiser, *The German Historicist Tradition*, 521–28.

8. See also my three-paragraph summary of this book by Dilthey in my study, *Religion and the Rise of History*, 225–26.

9. For recent, excellent, and full accounts of both Droysen and Dilthey and their

tee, Dilthey praised his "right satisfactory philosophical training" while Droysen praised his knowledge, his calm and understanding judgment, and concluded with the tribute, "In every respect flawless."

More than most studies on Hintze since the time of Hartung and Meisner, I emphasized not only the excellence of the traditional kind of training for a historian that Hintze received through the year 1884, but also why in 1885 he turned to new areas of study at the University of Berlin. From the fall of 1885 through the summer of 1888, he was registered as a student of law, and during these years, he studied law and especially, political economy. At this time, he became closely connected with Gustav Schmoller, and in 1888 he accepted a position as co-worker of a new and large publication known as the *Acta Borussica* or the collection and publication of documents of the Prussian state in the eighteenth century.

Gustav Schmoller was the heart and soul of this publication that came into being in 1887, and in October 1888, he was able to secure the services of Hintze for work on the silk industry in Prussia in the eighteenth century. In 1892, the results of four years of labor appeared in print with two volumes of documents and a third volume which was an account of the history of this industry in Prussia. As Heinrich Treitschke stated in 1895, this work was "a model accomplishment" (14). Most of all, however, I emphasized the statement by Schmoller in 1895 that Hintze possessed the most historical, literary, juristic, and *"staatswissenschaftliche"* education that he had ever encountered in a man of his age (20–21).

Hintze's history of the silk industry in Prussia was clearly work under the direction of Gustav Schmoller. One of the most useful parts of my dissertation is where I carefully traced, article by article, the development of Schmoller's contributions to Prussian economic, administrative, institutional, constitutional, and comparative studies from 1869 to 1900 (116–38). For Hintze, Schmoller was the real founder of Prussian constitutional and administrative history, for he was the one who really brought this to bloom (137). In both of these areas and in the development of comparative studies and a comparative method for the study of history, Hintze was Schmoller's greatest student and successor.

When Hintze agreed to work for the *Acta Borussica* for eight hours a day, he also agreed that he would not accept a university position (*Habilitation*) until the work of this publication had reached a certain point. Thus

---

significance for the theory of history, see Beiser, *The German Historicist Tradition*, 289–364 (Droysen, 289–321, Dilthey, 322–64).

it was not until August 1, 1895, when Hintze was 34 years old, that he was admitted to the faculty of the University of Berlin. One of the strengths of my dissertation was that from the beginning, I emphasized the significance of the close personal and professional relationship between Otto Hintze and Friedrich Meinecke for Western historical thought—a friendship that began in 1888 when they were both working in the Prussian archives. Another basic strength was how this friendship was linked with the two basic concepts of modern historical thought, for from the beginning of their friendship, they emphasized, discussed, and argued about the words *Individualität* and *Entwicklung* (development). Since up to the present time, the details of this story have laid unknown and unread in my dissertation from the year 1967, this chapter is the retelling of this story in one place and in a very condensed way.

Two of the best sources for Hintze's intellectual development are Meinecke's two autobiographical books: *Erlebtes 1862–1901*, which was first published in 1941; and *Strassburg/Freiburg/Berlin*, which was first published in 1949. Meinecke's description of their first meeting in the Prussian archives during their long apprenticeships, which I translated from his *Erlebtes 1862–1901*, is also a confirmation of the excellence of Hintze's training:

> As a new helper in the archives, I was sitting at my ancient writing table in the reading room when a very straight man with a brown face furrowed with dueling scars, entered the room. Without a glance of acknowledgement to me, or to the young official who was nominally in charge, he walked with measured steps to the documents which were ready for him. "*O dios*," the god-like, was the title which Krauske gave him. Krauske's conversation was like an effervescent waterfall. Hintze's words, and he did not like to enter into conversation, were like a broad and powerful stream under heavy cloud. His words were of compelling logic so that one could only criticize the premises now and then, but his words were always directed to the entirety of the matter. He was the best prepared and had the broadest views of us all. Never weak towards the outside, he was also hard like a knight even when he expressed tender inner feeling. One always had to make the first move towards any social activities, but then he went in good humor and often with splendid wit (19–20).

Before Hintze and Meinecke began their academic careers in the 1890's, they were very aware of the differences in their basic views concerning the nature of history. These differences became very obvious in a discussion between Hintze, Meinecke, and Krauske that Meinecke also reported in his *Erlebtes 1862–1901* (157).

> "There are no laws in history," explained Krauske once in our conversation. I agreed with him because at that time, I knew no other laws than those accepted in the natural sciences. "There are laws in history," Hintze replied just as firmly. Krauske called him "the evolutionist" (*Entwicklungsreiher*) because Hintze, as soon as he became enthusiastic, listed events as pieces of a great development only in order to amalgamate them immediately into a strong causative relationship. The individual life with its mysterious origin which Krauske and I loved, he pushed aside not without attention but because he did not consider it of primary value for research" (435).

Hintze and Meinecke continued their discussion of the question of whether history was collective or individualistic, and whether history was the work of collective and mass powers or of individual human beings, when they spent four weeks together in Switzerland in 1891. While Hintze stated that the trip helped to give him a stronger understanding of the individual, Meinecke confessed that he had received a warning not to exaggerate his basic tendency. Meinecke's conclusion was that such basic differences were the result of innate tendencies (435).

In 1893, two years after this discussion in Switzerland, Hintze demonstrated "his right philosophical training" when he presented his views concerning the nature of history, laws in history, the relationship between history and philosophy, and the philosophy of history in a review of Georg Simmel's *Die Probleme der Geschichsphilosophie* (1892). Here, Hintze demonstrated that he was not going to leave many basic questions concerning the theory of history to the philosophers of history, and that from the beginning, a philosophy of history was a part of his historical work (435–37).

In 1894, Wilhelm Windelband presented a lecture in Strassburg called "Geschichte und Naturwissenschaft"—a lecture that immediately became famous because it was a direct challenge to Dilthey's *Introduction to the Human Sciences*. While Carl Menger was most responsible for introducing into German economic thought the idea that the phenomenal world could either be regarded in its general aspect or in its concrete individual aspect, Wilhelm Windelband was most responsible for projecting this idea into the debate concerning the natural sciences, the human sciences, and history (162).

In this famous lecture, Windelband suggested that instead of distinguishing sciences on the basis of their content, it was better to distinguish them according to their cognitive goals (*Erkenntnisziele*). According to Windelband, there were two fundamental ways of dealing with subject matter: (1) the laying down of laws, in which case knowledge was "nomothetic"; and (2) the description of individual facts, in which case knowledge was "ideographic" (162). While Dilthey regarded psychology as the basis of the human sciences, Windelband regarded it as a nomothetic science that was naturalistic to the core. For Windelband, historical knowledge was concerned with the meaning of a particular incident or event in its concreteness, its individuality, or its uniqueness, for history was *ideographic*. While the tendency of thought of the natural sciences was toward abstraction, the tendency of historical thought was toward *Anschauulichkeit* or perception (162).[10]

In his "spirited" response,[11] Dilthey, certainly did list some of the disadvantages of Windelband's division of the sciences in accordance with these two different goals might have (162–63). For Dilthey, the basic ideal of the human sciences was "the understanding of the entire human-historical individuation." He was opposed to a sharp separation of the natural sciences and the human sciences on the basis of their interest in general laws or in particular historical facts. He insisted that the combination of the general and of "*Individuation*" was the real nature of the systematic human sciences, and if one really wanted to recognize reality, it was necessary to seek its characteristics in what was bound together by the nature of its content. If psychology was to be classified as a natural science which sought general laws, then he warned that most of the human sciences would also have to be considered as natural sciences. Thus, history alone would have to form the other class (163).

Even in the case of history, Dilthey thought it would be difficult to apply this abstract separation of goals to the work of Polybius, Machiavelli, Montesquieu, Tocqueville, Taine, or Nietzsche. Especially, he warned that there would be many disadvantages in separating history from the

---

10. For a recent, excellent, and full account of this lecture, its significance, for Windelband's "Clash with Dilthey," and for the significance of Windelband's work as a whole, see Beiser, *The German Historicist Tradition*, 365–92.

11. Ibid., 329.

systematic human sciences and in separating the general part of the human sciences from those which were directed toward the singular and comparison of the singular (163–64).

The views of Hintze and Meinecke concerning the nature of history became a matter of central importance for the guild of professional historians in Germany in 1895, when first Heinrich von Sybel died and then Heinich von Treitschke (1896), leaving Meinecke as the editor of the *Historische Zeitschrift*, the most famous and model professional journal for historians in the world at that time. One of the first things Meinecke did was to bring in his two friends, Krauske and Hintze, who for more than thirty years, supported Meinecke as co-workers in directing this influential journal.[12] According to Theodore Schieder, one of Meinecke's successors as editor of this journal, these years were the greatest period for this journal, since for most of this period, Meinecke could count on three outstanding scholars of very different background—Moritz Ritter, Ernst Troeltsch, and Otto Hintze.[13] From 1896 to 1931, some of Hintze's greatest articles were published in this journal.

One of the first tasks that Meinecke asked of his new co-worker was for Hintze to express his views about "individualistic" and "collectivistic" concepts of history in connection with the controversy raging over the work of Karl Lamprecht. In a short but significant article, which both Meinecke and Schieder considered the best that emerged out of this controversy (26), Hintze insisted that history could not be identified with a one-sided emphasis on an individualistic or a collectivistic approach (26). Where Hintze agreed most of all with Lamprecht was that historical scholarship needed to be placed "on the broad basis of thorough and profound research in social psychology." In one notable sentence, which characterized all of Hintze's work, he said: "To use a geographic metaphor, we want to know not only the ranges and summits, but also the base of the mountains; not merely the heights and depths of the surface, but the entire continental mass."[14]

---

12. Both of them joined Meinecke in 1896–97. Krauske continued until his death in 1930; Hintze continued until after the political change over in 1933; and Meinecke gave up the editorship under political pressure in 1935. Schieder, "Die deutsche Geschichtswissenschaft im Spiegel der Historischen Zeitschrift," 15. Hereafter this journal is cited as *HZ*.

13. Ibid., 26.

14. "The Individualist and the Collective Approach to History," *The Historical Essays of Otto Hintze*, 366.

While Hintze was very concerned about broadening traditional historical scholarship and was opposed to a sharp dichotomy between German idealism and Western European positivism, his friend Meinecke was very concerned about maintaining and developing the tradition of German idealism. He did not think that there was any need for a great change or for a "breakthrough" in philosophy, for he thought it was only necessary to go back to the point of departure of the historical movement of German idealism, which had never been dethroned by the movement of positivism. Although Meinecke recognized that Hintze had drawn near to the positivists on account of the depth and austerity of his historical views, he was accepted by his fellow historians who were attempting to revive the great traditions of Ranke and of German idealism. For Meinecke, it was important that Hintze respected "*das Geheimnis*" (the secret, or the unknown) in history.[15]

In the year 1902, Hintze wrote a letter to Meinecke in which he jokingly used two phrases that represented their different and basic viewpoints when he suggested that a certain action was probably bound to happen since "the decisive individuality" did not seem to be in direct contrast to "the general tendency of development" (452).[16] While Meinecke loved the word "individuality," Hintze loved to write about general tendencies of development; about one great process of development; about stages of development; about the way historians regarded development; and about the concept of development. While the concept of individuality was the basic concept for Meinecke's thought and work, the word "*Entwicklung*" and the concept of development were of basic importance for Hintze's thought and work (452–53).

In the year 1905, Heinrich Rickert (1863–1936), a philosopher of the same generation as Hintze and Meinecke, published a book called *Die Probleme der Geschichtsphilosophie*—a book that took up the ideas of Windelband concerning the division of the sciences and a book that Frederick C. Beiser called "the simplest and clearest account of his [Rickert's] distinction between the sciences."[17] In my brief summary and evaluation of Rickert's views on this subject in 1967 (164–72), one of the things that I emphasized was how Rickert continued the basic distinction that Wil-

---

15. Meinecke, *Strassburg/ Freiburg/ Berlin*, 155–56.

16. Letter from Hintze to Meinecke on July 2, 1902, Geheime Staatsarchiv Berlin, Rep. 92, Friedrich Meinecke (Nachlass), Meinecke-Korrespondenz, 15, Hintze, Blatt 336.

17. Ibid., 400.

delband had made between the nomothetic knowledge and method of the natural sciences, and the ideographic knowledge and method of history. Although Rickert continued to use these terms, which he inherited from his teacher, he preferred to speak about a "generalizing" method in contrast to an "individualizing" method (166).

Although (for Rickert) history was concerned with the unique and with individual phenomenon, this did not mean that historians could do without general concepts. It did mean, however, that such concepts were used as means rather than ends, for ideas such as church, state, class or culture were introduced into historical descriptions to define the individual phenomenon with which the historian was concerned (166–67). One of the main points of agreement between Rickert and Dilthey concerned the significance of values and value judgments for the human sciences and especially for history. In this respect, scholars agree, Rickert went way beyond what Dilthey had done, and in 1927, Otto Hintze credited Rickert with being the "actual founder of the historical theory of values."[18]

The reactions of Meinecke to Windelband's and Rickert's basic views are both interesting and very important. In his *Erlebtes 1862–1901*, Meinecke tells the story of how in his first semester (1882), he had the good fortune of taking Droysen's famous course on *Historik* and how Droysen and this course had a lasting impression on him. Although Meinecke regretted that he had not taken a course from Dilthey, he provides a good picture of him, for Dilthey was the professor who questioned Meinecke on philosophy at the time of Meinecke's doctoral examination in 1886.[19] In the 1890s or around the time that Meinecke became the editor of the *Historische Zeitschrift*, Meinecke reports that he was "captivated more and more" by Dilthey and sought in vain for his support for this journal (449). On the other hand, Meinecke reports that he greeted Windelband's famous lecture in 1894 as a declaration of war on positivism, which brought needed assistance for historians (449).

Meinecke's views of the nature and significance of Rickert's work in *Strassburg/Freiburg/Berlin* were also very positive, for here he emphasized how in the years before and after 1900, Rickert had transformed Windelband's ideas into a logical work of art, which provided a firm philosophical

---

18. Hintze, "Troeltsch and the Problems of Historicism," 406.

19. Meinecke, *Erlebtes*, 119–123. Here, Meinecke reports that the Predicate cum laude, that he was awarded on May 20, 1886, was awarded less frequently than at the time he was writing.

bulwark for the individual creative spirit (450). Certainly, the term and the idea of an "individualizing" method in contrast to a "generalizing" method were of great importance for Meinecke and his later view of the nature of historicism.

What about Hintze? From the year 1892 and throughout the rest of his career, Hintze reviewed many books dealing with history and theory, yet he did not review any books by Windelband or Rickert. However, in his essay in 1927 on "Troeltsch and the Problems of Historicism," Hintze demonstrated a thorough knowledge of Rickert's work and its significance for Ernst Troeltsch.

In the years 1905 and 1906, however, Hintze wrote two book reviews that clearly indicated his attitude toward Dilthey's foundational work. In 1905, Eduard Spranger (a student of Wilhelm Dilthey) wrote a book called *Die Grundlagen der Geschichtswissenschaften, eine erkenntnistheoretisch—psychologische Untersuchung*, a book that Hintze reviewed in the same year. One of the ideas that Hintze especially recommended in this very favorable review, was what Spranger had to say about "psychological-historical type-building." Hintze's conclusion was especially important, for here, he simply stated that he felt no call to take a critical position with regard to Spranger's epistemological discussion, since he was too close to the general view of this author to make any significant criticisms (438–39).

In 1906, in a very important five-page review of Simmel's important second edition (1905) of his *Die Probleme der Geschichtsphilosophie: Eine erknenntnistheoretische Studie*, Hintze credited Simmel for the epistemological foundation that was lacking in the first edition. He also thought Simmel's views concerning the concept of historical law were even more convincing with this new epistemological foundation. He also agreed with Simmel in placing "understanding" (*Verstehen*) in the center of operation by which our intellect produced historical pictures (460–61).

While Hintze agreed with Simmel's points concerning historical law as a contradiction in itself and the concept of the intellectual operation called "understanding," he was not satisfied with Simmel's conclusions concerning the success of attempts to grasp historical material conceptually by constructing types and composite personalities or by employing tendencies of development such as integration and differentiation (461). Here, Hintze presented his own views of the different ways historians discussed the idea of evolution, especially a catastrophic view and a more vegetative or gradual view of the life process (462–64).

Hintze was also concerned about the way Simmel dealt with the problem of objectivity. Although Hintze thought that Simmel had certainly demonstrated the subjective condition of historical writing, he was not satisfied with Simmel's views concerning "historical realism" or the way Simmel attacked the view that historical study was a mirror of occurrences as they actually happened (464–65). One of the important points that Hintze made about what one of my teachers liked to call "the reality principle," was how a respect for reality held the sovereign intellect of the historian in narrow boundaries; for the historian was not a "copyist" of reality but rather a "translator" (465).[20]

While this review should be of importance to Simmel scholars, its basic importance today is mainly for Hintze studies, for here, Hintze presented not only his most complete expression of his views concerning the concept of development before World War I, but he also expressed his view that the greatest difference among historians was in presentation. Hintze's defense of both Ranke's and Droysen's "objectivity" and their kinds of presentation is still important for historians today, but so is his discussion of how his own form of presentation differed from both of them (462–71).

One of Hintze's most significant statements that he made in regard to the question of objectivity and subjectivity for Ranke and Droysen was that the writing of history of his (Hintze's) day was a child of epistemological criticism, which had made the historian aware of the subjective picture that he presented. He did not know, he said, whether Ranke had thought much about epistemological problems, but he did know that Droysen had built his *Historik* on this idea; for Droysen's basic position was: "*Wie wird aus den Geschäften Geschichte*" (463).

Particularly where Hintze was discussing the nature of Ranke's, Droysen's, and his own forms of presentation (462–71), it is obvious that Hintze was following a tradition established by his teacher Droysen, who more than anyone else, thought through, taught, and discussed the different forms of historical presentation (466–72). According to Hintze, there were two main directions of historical interest that could be seen in the presentation of historians. In the first direction, the interest centered in reproducing a portion of past life, by way of research to understand (*forschend zu verstehen*), as Droysen explained it, or in order to awaken a feeling of sympathy (*Mitgefühl*) for its being, as Ranke explained it. This frame of mind was

---

20. See especially L. Smith, *Religion and the Rise of History*, 220 and this whole paragraph emphasizing the importance of this book review by Hintze.

mainly epic as it narrated, described, and characterized. This was the main kind of history writing by the great historians of antiquity and of modern times (466).

In the other direction, however, the past was considered more as the conditions preceding the present. This viewpoint did not really narrate "what really happened," but explained how it came to be (*"wie es geworden ist"*). This viewpoint was more didactic and really stood in closer connection to a conceptual discipline such as political science or political economy. The first direction or viewpoint naturally commanded a higher degree of objectivity than the latter, for it followed more closely the manuscripts and the threads of the great happenings, which proceeded from the actions of single persons or also from the masses. This second viewpoint required a more sovereign treatment of the material since it was more concerned with conditions than with happenings, more with the life of the masses than with the life of the individual, and more with institutions than with actions (467).

Both viewpoints assumed causal relationships, but while the historian of the former direction pointed out such connections when they were apparent, the historian of the second viewpoint was satisfied when he could present an interrelated development showing the origins of the present out of the past and making it understandable to a certain degree. For Hintze, historical laws could not be ascertained by either of these directions (467–68).

In addition to artistic presentations of the past, which, like Ranke, sought to awaken a sympathetic feeling for the ages of humanity, Hintze thought there was a "purely scientific" (*rein wissenschaftlich*) conception which sought to explain historically what had come to be. The more one sought to isolate one subject out of the bundle of historical disciplines called history, the clearer it became that the goal of the historian could not be to awaken a sympathetic feeling for the past. Even though he thought that might sound rationalistic, he suggested that the goal of the historian was to explain the present out of the past, to connect the present to the past and to former times, and to learn to understand the present as a historical product that was a cross section of development. In the last instance, Hintze thought the real effort of the historian had to be to present the connection between past and present and to understand the distances involved (470–71).

At this time, both Hintze and Meinecke were working diligently on their new forms of historical presentation. While Hintze was developing a broad comparative approach to the study of Western "Constitutional and Administrative History," as all Anglophone readers can see in the four essays before World War I that Gilbert translated in 1975, Meinecke was working on a book that became a sensation when it was published in 1907. Indeed, Meinecke's *Weltbürgertum und Nationalstaat (Cosmopolitanism and the National State)* was one of the first major contributions to the development of twentieth-century intellectual history. With this volume, Meinecke transformed political historiography into the history of ideas,[21] and here he clearly demonstrated his ability to link "ideas and men."

In this second autobiographical writing, Meinecke also reported the marriage of his fifty-one-year-old friend to Hedwig Guggenheimer, a twenty-eight-year-old student of his who was also interested in a career in history. One of the things about this marriage that Meinecke emphasized was that this was a new kind of academic marriage, for in their elegant and childless apartment, both Otto and Hedwig Hintze pursued their own lines of work in their own separate studies. The other thing that Meinecke stressed was that perhaps this marriage saved Hintze's life, for Meinecke thought that Hintze hardly knew how to take care of himself when he was very sick before his marriage (63).[22]

In the momentous year 1914, Hintze became a member of the Royal Prussian Academy of Sciences and delivered his "*Eintrittsrede*" or "Inaugural Address." This short document, which I included as an appendix in my dissertation in 1967 and which is translated into English as an appendix to this work, is both indispensable for Hintze studies and the best place for a student interested in Hintze's work as a whole to begin. In 1914, Hintze was best known as the outstanding historian of the Prussian state, and today he is still recognized as the main successor to both Droysen and Ranke in the field of Prussian history (172–84). In this speech, Hintze pointed out that from the beginning, it was not a part of his goal to write a history of the Prussian state. Yet, two of the strengths of my dissertation were that it showed not only how Hintze became the outstanding authority on Prussian history in the twentieth century, but also how, as Hintze stated in this speech, Prussia became a "paradigm" for his study of the modern Western state.

21. Antoni, "From History to Sociology," 92.
22. Meinecke, *Strassburg/ Freiburg/ Berlin*, 154–55.

The Expert's Historian

From 1910 to 1914, Hintze was working on a request that he believed he could not refuse: to write an official history of the Hohenzollerns in Brandenburg-Prussia in connection with their five-hundredth anniversary celebration in 1915. Although *Die Hohenzollern und ihr Werk: Fünfhundert Jahre vaterländischer Geschichte* (1915) was a large work (703 pages), it was an immediate success, for one ten-thousand-copy edition followed after the other (405). Further, although it was an official history, it demonstrated a depth of knowledge and a striving for truth that characterized all of Hintze's work.

The year 1914 was also a very important year for Hintze and Meinecke, both personally and professionally, because shortly after the outbreak of World War I, Hintze had the opportunity to welcome Meinecke to the faculty of the University of Berlin. Hintze now also had the opportunity to nominate Meinecke for membership in the Royal Prussian Academy of Sciences, which was one of his first functions as a new member of this body. Unlike most selections for this Academy, Meinecke was elected for membership without any opposing votes being cast (446). In the next year, Meinecke and Hintze began taking walks on every other Sunday—a practice that Meinecke was able to continue until the summer of 1943.

The year 1915 is an important one for the history of the *Historismus* debate and the German historicist tradition. First of all, in Meinecke's "*Eintrittsrede*" or Inaugural Address to the Prussian Academy of Sciences in 1915, he reported how increasingly, his interest had shifted from personalities to ideas and to two major tasks. The first, he said, was "to understand the transformation in the nature of politics since the days of the Renaissance," and the other was "to investigate the rise of our modern concept of history [*Geschichtsauffassung*]."[23] These were the subjects of Meinecke's last two large intellectual histories, both of which were important events for the *Historismus* debate.

Secondly, and most importantly for this story, this was the year Ernst Troeltsch began his career as a professor of philosophy at the University. Thus, in this year, Meinecke had the pleasure of nominating Troeltsch for membership in the Royal Prussian Academy of Sciences. As a result, the two-way dialogue between Hintze and Meinecke concerning the nature of history and the concept of individuality and development became a three-way discussion or debate.

---

23. Smith, *Religion and the Rise of History*, 239.

As Editor of the *Historische Zeitschrift*, Meinecke generously gave his new co-worker the opportunity to publish one article after another in this journal. In 1922, these articles were joined together to form much of a large work with the important title, *Der Historismus und seine Probleme*. When this volume was first published, this title was supposed to be the title for a two-volume work, and this first volume was called *Das logische Problem der Geschichtsphilosophie*. Since Dilthey was not able to write or publish a second volume before his death in 1923, however, this single volume has been known by its collective title.

In these articles and this volume, and during the last years of his life, Troeltsch struggled valiantly to free the term *"Historismus"* from the negative meanings it had up to this time. For Troeltsch, *Historismus* "is to be completely disconnected from the bad secondary meaning and to be understood in the sense of *the fundamental historicizing of all our thinking about human beings, its culture, and its values.*"[24] It is significant that this student of Windelband, who came out of the Windelband-Richert school, dedicated this work both to Wilhelm Dilthey and to Wilhelm Rickert, since for Troeltsch, "the logic of history needed to be deeply rooted in *historical reality* itself" and also "had to be the *formal logic of history*."[25] Therefore, Troeltsch proposed to work out the formal logic of history "from what the historian actually practices."[26]

One of the most important achievements by Troeltsch in this work was to list and discuss eleven categories or concepts "with which the historian actually works in historical investigations."[27] Of these eleven basic concepts or categories, which Toshima Yasukata conveniently lists for us, "those of 'individual totality (*individuelle Totalität*) and 'development' (*Entwicklung*) are fundamental and pivotal, and the rest are corollary." Here Yasukata makes an additional and very important point: "It should be pointed out that Troeltsch deliberately coined the term 'individual totality' to replace the commonly used term 'individuality.'"[28] Thus, for Troeltsch, the proper subjects of scientific history were "collective individualities," such as

---

24. Troeltsch, *Der Historismus und seine Probleme*, 102. Here, I have used the translation of Toshima Yasukata, *Ernst Troeltsch, Systematic Theologian of Radical Historicality* (Atlanta: Scholars Press, 1986), 127. See also, Troeltsch's other definition of this term translated by Yasukata on this same page.

25. Yasukata, *Ernst Troeltsch*, 130.

26. Ibid.

27. Ibid., 131.

28. Ibid.

"peoples, states, classes, social ranks, cultural communities, religious communities, and complex occurrences of all kinds, such as wars, revolutions and so forth."[29] Also for Troeltsch, as Yasukata explains, "Thus understood, the concept of individuality, however, already implies the second basic concept of development."[30] According to Robert J. Rubanowice, Troeltsch "devoted more space in *Historicism and Its Problems* to an explication of the meaning of historical development than to the other ten categories combined."[31]

After the death of Troeltsch in 1923, the public debate between Meinecke and Hintze concerning the nature of historicism began. In that year, Meinecke affirmed his position by emphasizing "the primacy of the idea of individuality" over the idea of development both for the rise of historicism in Germany and for Troeltsch.[32] In the following year, the term "*Historismus*" was a basic one in Meinecke's *Die Idee der Staatsräson*, for here he emphasized how around the beginning of the nineteenth century, an intellectual revolution took place in Germany. To Meinecke, this revolution was "perhaps the greatest revolution in thought experienced by the West" and he associated it with the terms "idealism" and "*Historismus*."[33]

In 1927, Meinecke made another major contribution to the historicism debate when he asked Hintze to write an essay for the *Historische Zeitschrift* about their departed friend's very significant work, *Der Historismus und seine Probleme*. Just as Hintze's 1897 essay, "The Individualist and the Collective Approach to History," was the best writing that emerged out of the whole "Lamprecht Controversy," so Hintze's 1927 essay, "Troeltsch and the Problems of Historicism: Critical Studies," was the best essay that emerged out of this foundational period for the term "*Historismus*."

Thus far in my life, I have told the story of this historicism debate between Troeltsch, Meinecke, and Hintze at two different times (in 1967, 432–503 and in 2009, 237–47), but it is still basically an unknown story. Perhaps a third time might help historians recognize the importance of this story for their profession, for it is the story not only of the discovery of the

---

29. Ibid.

30. Ibid.

31. Rubanowice, *The Crisis in Consciousness*, 86. For a good summary of each of these eleven categories, see pp. 80–89.

32. L. Smith, *Religion and the Rise of History*.

33. Meinecke, *Machiavellism*.

term "*Historismus*" as a basic term for modern historical thought, but also of the discovery of historicism as a method of inquiry.

One of the very important things to note about Gilbert's introductory remarks to his translation of Hintze's essay, "Troeltsch and the Problems of Historicism: Critical Studies," is the fact that this essay included not only the ideas in the book, *Der Historismus und Seine Probleme*, "but also Troeltsch's views presented in a collection of essays, *Deutcher Geist und Westeuropa*, and in lectures published under the title *Der Historismus und seine Überwindung* (in English translation, *Christian Thought: Its History and Application*)."[34]

Secondly, Gilbert rightly points out that "Hintze's essay transcends the purpose of discussing Troeltsch's ideas," that "it has a wider scope," and that "it provides a general statement on historical theory."[35]

Thirdly, in this article, Hintze resumes discussion of the questions that he treated in his earlier work "The Individualist and the Collective Approach to History," but his treatment in this later study "is more comprehensive and systematic."[36]

Fourthly, Gilbert added, "It includes an examination of the validity of the attempts of the philosopher Heinrich Rickert and his school to separate the methods of the cultural sciences from those of the natural sciences; it examines the usefulness of Max Weber's sociological ideas for the work of the historian; it considers the significance of Spengler's notions for the writing of comparative history; and it probes not only Troeltsch's ideas on historicism, but also those of Hintze's Berlin colleagues and friends, Friedrich Meinecke and Eduard Spranger."[37] For these and other reasons, it is difficult to see how most Anglophone historians and philosophers since 1927 could ignore this essay, for it is still of basic importance for both of these disciplines.

In my study called *Religion and the Rise of History*, I focused on four main problems that Hintze had with Troeltsch's views of historicism, especially in his book *Der Historismus und seine Probleme*. First of all, Hintze pointed out that it "leads again and again down the path of skepticism and relativism that Troeltsch hoped to close off." Secondly, Troetlsch had not

---

34. "Troeltsch and the Problems of Historicism: Critical Studies." *The Historical Essays of Otto Hintze*, 368.
35. Ibid.
36. Ibid.
37. Ibid.

made a sharp and clear distinction between historicism as a methodology and as a *Weltanschauung*. Thirdly, for Hintze, there was as yet "no precise demarcation of the area covered by the concept of historicism. Fourthly, Hintze criticized Troeltsch "for having no interest whatsoever in psychological methods."[38]

In addition to what I wrote in connection with each of these four points, however, is the fundamental importance of several additional statements that Hintze made in this essay in relation to the history of modern historical thought. At the beginning of the section called "Historical Logic and Value Systems," Hintze made a statement that is of fundamental importance for modern historical thought: "Following in the footsteps of Rickert's pioneering work on historical logic, Troeltsch undertook a logical analysis of the phenomenon he described as 'the historization of our thought on human affairs.'" Here, it was significant that Hintze credited Troeltsch for discussing "the two concepts of specifically historical thought: the concept of individuality and that of development" (490).[39]

It is especially this section (381–91) of this translated Hintze essay that should be included in an anthology of writings by great historians, for after Hintze explains how these two concepts are the two concepts of specifically historical thought, this section culminates with his definition of historicism (390). Before Hintze explained how these two concepts were based on two simple analogies that historians use in constituting historical objects, Hintze made a very important statement concerning the possible and actual object of history. Since Gilbert did not translate this distinction correctly, here I want to quote my emphasis on this distinction in my dissertation in 1967:

> In constituting an historical object, Hintze thought that a distinction had to be made between the possible object of history and actual objects of history. The latter was a problem for the individual historian, but the former was one of importance for historical logic. He suggested that history could have as its possible object or subject "everything that belonged to human culture and which was related to a perception of time." For this, he thought the concept of individual totality played a decisive role. As a decisive criterion for establishing such a historical totality, he suggested

---

38. Smith, *Religion and the Rise of History*, 141–42
39. Ibid., 242.

that it was the possibility of comprehending the totality as a "unit of life" (*Lebenseinheit*).⁴⁰

Since Hintze's distinction between possible object of history and actual objects of history is so important for both the theory and the practice of history, and since this section of this particular essay—in addition to an English translation of his Inaugural Address to the Prussian Royal Academy in 1914—should be included in any future anthology of selections from great historians, here is a correction that could be used either in such a work or in a new edition of Gilbert's book.

> In defining objects of historical study, one must distinguish between the possible object of history and the actual objects of history. The latter is overall no problem for philosophy or even the logic of history. Which object the historian selects to research and to present, however, depends on several factors: the historian's personal interest, the need for work in a given area, and the nature and accessibility of source material. These factors, however, have no significance for the philosophy of history and would be of importance only for a specialized theory of historical methods. Possible object of history, however, is everything that belongs to human culture and that is viewed from a perspective of time. The concept of the individual totality is, of course, crucial to determining an object of historical study, and I would suggest that the only decisive criterion for defining an individual totality is its comprehensibility as a unit of life [*Lebenseinheit*]. Troeltsch used this phrase, but he did not ascribe to it the significance it has. The defining of objects of historical study is, in my opinion, an act of intuitive, not rational thought. The historian's thinking here is not logical but analogical. The concept of the individual personality underlies this analogical thinking and has, I believe, a much greater significance for history than Troeltsch allows it.⁴¹

The three important things to note about this translation in comparison to that of Gilbert, are, first and most of all, that the distinction between

---

40. Smith, "Otto Hintze's Comparative Constitutional History of the West," 491–92. Because of the significance of this passage, here I quoted the original German passage in a footnote: "Mögliches Gegenstand der Geschichte ist alle, was zur menschlichen Kultur gehört und der zeitanschauung untersteht." Hintze, "Troeltsch und die Probleme des Historismus, *GA*, 2: 341. In addition, when Gilbert quotes Hintze in the following phrase—"Any aspect of a past human society, viewed from a perspective of time, can be an object of historical study"—Hintze would not have included the word "past."

41. Hintze, "Troeltsch and the Problems of Historicism," 385.

"the possible object" and actual objects is much more clear; for Hintze did not say, "Possible objects present no problem for the philosophy or even the logic of history." Secondly, Hintze did not say, "any aspect of past human society," for here the word "past" is inserted by the translator and is not consistent with Hintze's view of the nature of history. Thirdly, I have inserted the German word "*Lebenseinheit*" in brackets because of its great importance for Hintze, both for the theory and practice of history.

For Hintze, just as the actual object of an historian is grasped intuitively as a *Lebenseinheit*, so the category of "development" offers "a close parallel to this"; for here "the historical object appears in motion, not at rest."[42] After offering a brilliant explanation how the category of development provides "simply one more aspect of the object in addition to that offered by the category of individuality,"[43] he explains how, just as the category of individuality is based on the analogy of a *Lebenseinheit*, so the category of development is based on an analogy of the "*Lebensprozess*."[44]

In my dissertation in the year 1967, I translated Hintze's definition of historicism in the following way:

> Historicism is a "new, unique, categorical-structure of the human spirit for the comprehension of historical things. It had formed gradually since the eighteenth century in the West and it had attained decisive significance in the nineteenth century, especially in Germany though not in Germany alone. It was characterized by the categories of individuality and development according to the analogies of a unit of life and a process of life. In contrast to the long dominant direction of thought based on the rationality which originated out of the view of the individual consciousness, this categorical structure was based on the powerful idea of a general life which was higher than individual reason and which in its entirety included the individual human being" (493–94).

The main advantage and disadvantage of this translation, like Gilbert's translation in *The Historical Essays of Otto Hintze* in 1975 (390) as compared to my 2009 translation in *Religion and the Rise of History* (242–43), are that it doesn't include the key German words in brackets.

---

42. Ibid., 388.
43. Ibid.
44. Hintze, "Troeltsch und die Probleme des Historismus," 341.

Because of the great significance of Hintze's definition of historicism for all of my thought and work for almost fifty years, here, I am also including my translation in 2009. That is, what one now calls historicism:

> is a new, unique, categorical structure of the mind [*des Geistes*] that began to arise in the West in the eighteenth century and achieved authoritative currency in the nineteenth, particularly in Germany, though not in Germany alone. It is characterized by the categories of individuality and development, which postulate a view of historical reality based on the analogy of the life unit [*Lebenseinheit*] and the life-process [*Lebensprozess*]."[45]

This translation was based not only on the translation in my dissertation in the year 1967 (393–94), but also on Gilbert's translation in *The Historical Essays of Otto Hintze* (390). One of the main problems that I have with Gilbert's translation is that he translates *"Lebenseinheit* as "unity of life," for in doing so, he gives this word a different meaning.

To show the significance of this definition of historicsm for the idea of history since the time of Kant, I want to repeat what I wrote in *Religion and the Rise of History* following my translation of this definition.

> Both chronologically and logically, this was a brilliant statement, for here, Hintze combined a picture of the rise and full development of historicism with the formal philosophy of Kant, with Dilthey's emphasis on psychology, and with Droysen's emphasis on history as a *Wissenschaft* and as a methodology based on the concept of time. When Hintze stated that the concepts of individuality and development should be regarded "formally" as "categorical structures of the human mind," he was supplementing Kant's (and Droysen's) two basic forms of *"innere Anschauung,"* for to Hintze "space and time were the constituent elements of all historical phenomena." When Hintze argued that historical thinking was basically analogical and that historicism was based on the two basic analogies that historians use to understand historical objects, he was both supplementing Dilthey's terminology and demonstrating his teacher's views concerning the importance of psychological understanding for all of the human sciences. When Hintze emphasized that "history could have as its possible object everything dealing with human culture in relation to a perception of time," and when he defined historicism as a method of inquiry and understanding, he was also supplementing Droysen's basic methodological principles. And when Hintze insisted that

---

45. Smith, *Religion and the Rise of History*, 242–43.

historicism should be defined in a "purely epistemological" way and that it was only another mode of thought or another set of methodological categories, he was articulating and supplementing the German understanding of history since the time of Chladenius—the idea of a *Geschichtswissenschaft*.

The end of this debate between Hintze and Meinecke concerning the nature and significance of historicism, came in 1936 with the publication of Meinecke's third main intellectual history, *Die Entstehung des Historismus*. In his preliminary remarks to this large, famous, and influential history, Meinecke explained how historicism was nothing else but the application to the historical world of the life-governing principles achieved by the great German movement from Leibniz to the death of Goethe."[46] In contrast to Hintze, however, Meinecke insisted that historicism was more than just a method of the human sciences, for life and the world appeared differently when one had become accustomed to viewing things in this new way. For Meinecke, the essence of historicism "is the substitution of a process *individualising* observation for a *generalizing* view of human forces in history."[47] This did not mean "that the historical method excludes altogether any attempt to find general laws in human life," he said, but it had to "make use of this approach and blend it with a feeling for the individual."[48] For Meinecke, the sense of individuality was something new that historicism created.

Although in the next few years, Meinecke wrote several essays that were supplements to this—his third and last great intellectual history—for all practical purposes, the publication of this work in 1936 can be seen as the end of the debate between Hintze and Meinecke concerning the nature of modern historical thought. Since World War II, the *Historismus* dialogue between Troeltsch, Hintze, and Meinecke has blossomed into a large and apparently endless one for historians in Germany,[49] while many history teachers and students in the United States are blissfully unaware of a dialogue that can be seen (though in retrospect) as the most significant one in the twentieth century concerning the nature of modern historical thought.[50]

46. Meinecke, *Historism*, iv.
47. Ibid., (emphasis in the original)
48. Ibid.
49. See my fairly lengthy summary of some representative studies on this subject in my study, *Religion and the Rise of History*, 245.
50. Ibid.

Meinecke, Troeltsch, Hintze, and the Discovery

One of the reasons that the *Historismus* debate was of major significance for the idea of history in the twentieth century is its significance for what H. Stuart Hughes called "the reconstruction" or the "reorientation" of European social thought, in his book *Consciousness and Society: The Reconstruction of European Social Thought 1890-1930* (1958). Although I used this book frequently to show Hintze's significance for this "reconstruction" in my dissertation in the year 1967, thus far I have seen no references to this story either in English or in German. Therefore in 2009, I used this book again for the same purpose, but here, I told this story in a much more compact, clear, and succinct way. Since I have not seen anyone else refer to the strong claims that I have made in either of these studies, I will try once more to use Hughes to provide the setting for Hintze's significance for the theory and practice of history.

Hughes claimed that "it was Germans and Austrians and French and Italians—rather than Englishmen or Americans or Russians—who in general, provided the fund of ideas that seem characteristic of our time."[51] For Hughes, Sigmund Freud was the towering figure of the generation of the 1890s. Just behind him came such figures as Benedetto Croce, Emile Durkheim, Vilfredo Pareto, Henri Bergson, Georges Sorel, Carl Jung, Friedrich Meinecke, and Ernst Troeltsch."[52]

In this study, Hughes showed how the leading social thinkers came to grips with Marxism, but most of all, he showed how the great intellectual conflict within the *Geisteswissenschaften*—or within those disciplines concerned with what Dilthey called "social-historical reality"—was between the idealist and the positivist traditions. According to Hughes, the decade of the 1890s was a "revolt against positivism," or the "whole tendency to discuss human behavior in terms of analogies drawn from natural science."[53]

Despite the facts (1) that here, Hughes was more concerned with European sociologists and social thought than with historians and historical thought, (2) that Meinecke was the only professional historian to receive considerable attention in Hughes' study, and (3) that Hintze was not mentioned, this excellent intellectual history provides a helpful framework for understanding the significance of Meinecke and Hintze for Western social-historical thought.

---

51. Hughes, *Consciousness and Society*, 13.
52. Ibid., 10-20.
53. Ibid., 37.

The Expert's Historian

For Hughes, Wilhelm Dilthey was a "great precursor" of this generation of the 1890s, for his work represented "the first thorough-going and sophisticated confrontation of history with positivism and natural science";[54] and here, he showed how Croce, Troeltsch, and Meinecke were important heirs of Dilthey. What separated Croce and Meinecke, Hughes argued, was a divergent interpretation of Dilthey's legacy. Both of them, he said, had narrowed their common inheritance. Neither had grasped the full importance of Dilthey's analysis of the interrelationships among the different branches of human study, nor had resumed the attempt to bring history into dynamic accord with social science; and each was too exclusively absorbed in preserving the newly won autonomy of historical study. Finally, both had failed to see that the relativist implications of Dilthey's thought might not necessarily threaten the whole notion of *Historismus*. I did not occur to them to revise the idealist theory of values within a frankly relativist framework. These were the great tasks that still remained if the intellectual revolution of the 1890s was to be pushed to its furthest limits.[55]

After I had quoted this passage from Hughes in my dissertation in 1967, I wrote the following words: "This, however, was not true of Hintze. It was precisely in these areas that he went beyond Meinecke and Croce in advancing the intellectual revolution of the 1890's; it was precisely in these areas that Hintze advanced the intellectual heritage of Dilthey" (452).

In my study *Religion and the Rise of History* in 2009, this same quotation was followed by these words: "Each of these things that Croce and Meinecke failed to accomplish, however, were accomplished by Hintze, especially in the article "Troeltsch and the Problems of Historicism" in 1927.

Both in 1967 and 2009, however, I discussed Hintze's work also in relation to that of Max Weber, and in both places this discussion took place in connection with the development of Historical Ideal Types, which is the subject of the next chapter.

---

54. Ibid.
55. Hughes, *Consciousness and Society*, 247–48.

3

Otto Hintze and Max Weber
From the Roots of Bureaucracy to the Invention of Historical Ideal Types

THREE OF HINTZE'S GREATEST contributions to the theory and practice of history were the three historical ideal types that he published from 1929 to 1931: (1) "Wesen und Verbreitung des Feudalismus" (1929)[1] or "The Nature and Spread of Feudalism," (2) "Typologie der ständischen Verfassungen des Abendlandes" (1930)[2] or " Typology of the Estates Constitutions of the Occident," and (3) "Wesen und Wandlung des Modernen Staates" (1931),[3] or "The Nature and Transformation of the Modern State." One of the reasons that these three essays are very significant both for the theory and the practice of history is that in the second of these articles, Hintze was the first German historian to use the term "typology."[4] These essays are also of fundamental importance for Western historical thought because from the beginning, these three kinds or types of Western institutional, structural, and/or constitutional development were of central importance

---

1. Hintze, "Wesen und Verbreitung des Feudalismus," 84–119.

2. Hintze, "Typologie der ständischen Verfassungen," 120–139. This essay was first published in *Historische Zeitschrift* 141 (1930) 1–47.

3. Hintze, "Wesen und Wandlung," 470–96.

4. Schieder, "Der Typus in der Geschichtswisssenschaft," 176 (71). This number in parenthesis, as in the previous chapter and the rest of this chapter, signifies where this information can be found in Smith, "Otto Hintze's Comparative Constitutional History of the West."

for his chief goal and work: a "Comparative Constitutional History of the West." Together they form a complete and unsurpassed typology of Western institutional development.

In the year 1897, Hintze first indicated the importance of these three constitutional types for the West as a whole, both as a unique individuality and as development. He did this in a programmatic essay called "Roschers politische Entwicklungstheorie."[5] As in so many of his most thought-provoking articles that were to follow, Hintze used a review of someone's work as the take-off point for the development of his own ideas. In this review of Wilhelm Roscher's *Politik: Geschichtliche Naturlehre der Monarchie, Aristokratie und Demokratie*, Hintze convincingly demonstrated that Roscher's six types of state forms based on the three Aristotelian forms mentioned in the title of his book, could not explain the different political and social development of all times and all peoples (213–18).[6]

This essay of 1897 was a programmatic essay because first of all, this is where Hintze first announced his two main academic and life goals: a general comparative constitutional history of the West and a study called *Politik* (376). Secondly, and most importantly for this study, in an essay that Reinhard Bendix abridged and had translated into English under the title "The State in Historical Perspective," one can find a very sophisticated account of Western institutional or constitutional development in essay form. This is an account that only Hintze could have written. As Bendix rightly emphasized, Hintze demonstrates the significant extent to which the structure of societies is shaped by external relations between states. "Taking into account both sources of change, external and internal, he sketches in bold strokes, but with fine historical scholarship, the forging of the nation state from its remote antecedents in Greek antiquity and in the Roman Empire."[7]

In this essay, Hintze was looking for "the types" that emerged between the city-state of antiquity and the modern nation states."[8] It is significant that when Hintze discusses how the municipal form of organization disappeared for a long time, he emphasizes that it was replaced by the "feudal type, which had already been prepared by the economic, administrative,

---

5. Hintze, "Roscher's politische Entwicklungstheorie," 3–45. This was a review of Wilhelm Roscher, *Geschichtliche Naturlehre der Monarchie, Aristokratie, und Demokratie*, 2nd ed.

6. Hintze's critical review of Roscher's *Politik* really began in 1895 with a review of this work in the *Historische Zeitschrift* 65 (1895) 96–99.

7. Bendix, ed., "Introduction" to "The State in Historical Perspective," 153.

8. Hintze, "The State in Historical Perspective," 157.

and military foundations of the declining Roman Empire."⁹ Here, he also discusses the emergence of "the feudal military system."¹⁰

For Hintze, the Roman church symbolized "the spiritual and religious unity of the West,"¹¹ but it was the "unique development of both the estate and monarchical principles" that "distinguishes the states which emerged from the social institution of the Western church from all other states in the world. If we compare the political structures of the Romano-Germanic peoples with other culture areas—for example, the areas of the Orthodox Church or of Islam—then the difference becomes readily apparent. A politically privileged nobility, one element of the estate principle, developed neither in Russia nor Turkey, though both had a special kind of feudalism."¹²

One of the basic themes of this essay and all of Hintze's work as a whole was "how the various stages of the states' external development corresponded to their internal structure. Thus, the structure of the small territorial state was of the estate-type (*ständisch*), but with the transition from the aggregated territorial state to the unified modern state, there usually emerged absolute monarchy."¹³ The emphasis of this essay, however, was not on feudalism or on the large, modern nation state, but on the nature and significance of the European territorial states with their *ständische* constitutions. For Hintze, "the representative system, until now has been the only way for large modern states to let people participate in government."¹⁴

This essay, translated from Hintze's programmatic essay, "Roschers politische Entwicklungstherorie," was just one of Bendix's important contributions to Hintze scholarship in the twentieth century. It is very important that this leading Max Weber scholar was also a Hintze scholar and did what he could to promote a knowledge of Hintze's work. One of the areas where Bendix brilliantly combined his knowledge of both Weber and Hintze—the two greatest scholars for the study of Western bureaucracy in the first third of the twentieth century—is his excellent article called "Bureaucracy" in the *International Encyclopedia of the Social Sciences* in 1968. The article that Bendix selected to use from Hintze is the one that I emphasized in my dissertation as a highpoint in Hintze's study of Western bureaucracy.

9. Ibid., 158.
10. Ibid.
11. Ibid., 159.
12. Ibid., 160.
13. Ibid., 166.
14. Ibid., 167.

The Expert's Historian

In chapter 5 of "Otto Hintze's Comparative Constitutional History of the West"—a chapter called "Administrative History and Constitutional History: The Development of Bureaucracy and the Bureaucratic State"—I argued first of all, that German scholarship led the way for the comparative analysis of modern bureaucracy in the West. While Gustav Schmoller was "the greatest pioneer in this development in the last decades of the nineteenth century," and while Max Weber was the greatest social scientist in this development in the first decades of the twentieth century, Otto Hintze was the greatest historian for the understanding of the historical development of European bureaucracy in the first decades of the twentieth century (338).

Most of Hintze's comparative studies in the first years of the twentieth century were related to his great introductory presentation of the governmental organization and general administration of Prussia around the year 1740, which was published by the *Acta Borussica in 1901*. This volume was the key volume for the entire *Acta Borussica* and is still one of the most impressive works in the institutional history of the eighteenth century, for it was a very penetrating study that was the result of almost a decade of research in the Prussian archives. It was a cross-sectional study that Hintze referred to as a description of conditions at a certain point of time rather than a constitutional and administrative history (27).

As Hintze explained to the Royal Prussian Academy in his "Entrance Address" in 1914: "In an introductory volume I sought by means of a cross-sectional study to give a penetrating and comprehensive presentation of the constitution and administration of the Prussian state around the year 1740. In so doing, I came to the conclusion that the distinction between the regional [*landschaftlich*] territorial and of the great state type in organs and institutions provided a particularly fruitful point of view. This distinction, which had seldom been employed up to that time, leads immediately into the core of the problem of the origin of absolutism and its creation, the modern military great state."[15] For Hintze, it was clear that the driving principle behind this change was the idea of power.

In the first sentence of this large volume in 1901, Hintze stated that in 1740, the Prussian monarchy was still not a completely unified state, for only in diplomatic language was the term "Prussia" used for the entire monarchy. For this transitional condition when Prussia was neither a

---

15. See the Appendix of this book.

simple territorial unit nor a modern military great state, Hintze adopted the term "composite (*zusammengesetze*) territorial state."

This was the basic study that was behind those classic "comparative and administrative" studies that Gilbert translated in *The Historical Essays of Otto Hintze*: "The Formation of States and the Constitutional Development: A Study of History and Politics" (1902); "Military Organization and the Organization of the State" (1906); "The Origins of the Modern Ministerial System: A Comparative Study" (1908); and "The Commissary and His Significance in General Administrative History: A Comparative Study" (1910, not 1919 as Gilbert mistakenly asserts). These essays have greatly influenced the study of Western bureaucracies since their publication.

Each of these five essays is a classic study dealing with basic aspects of European institutional development. Together, the essays demonstrate how Hintze already was a master of the comparative method well before World War I, and how important Prussia was for him for an understanding of many of the basic institutions of the modern Western state. Additionally, the essays reveal why Hintze can be regarded as one of the great ones in the discipline for his contributions to so many areas of Prussian and European history. While here, I want to mention that the first of these essays was most like the article that Bendix called "The State in Historical Perspective" and that continued to explore the relationship between the three main types of Western constitutions that developed within Latin Christendom—western feudalism, the "*ständische*" or the "estates constitutions," and the "great national unitary states."[16] The one essay that I want to emphasize here, however, is Hintze's brilliant essay written in the year 1911, which he called "Der Beamtenstand,"[17] In some ways this study can be considered as the high point of Hintze's work concerning the study of Prussian and Western bureaucracy.

In the first place, this study was unusual for that time in that it dealt with bureaucracy not as an instrument of the state, but rather with bureaucracy as a professional group[18] (357). At this time, Hintze believed that the study of bureaucracy as a social phenomenon had not received much attention since it was a subject that bordered on several disciplines. Historians, for instance, were most concerned with German and Prussian administrative organization with an emphasis on political rather than social

---

16. Hintze, "The Formation of States and Constitutional Development," 175.
17. Hintze, "Der Beamtenstand," 66–125.
18. Ibid., 66.

questions. Hintze suggested that a consideration of this subject would only be fruitful within a large "comparative social-historical framework."[19] In discussing bureaucracy within such a framework, he first considered the nature of modern bureaucracy, then its development, and finally the tendencies of development and the problems of the present. This was the basic organization of this pioneer study.

In the first section, Hintze stated that in considering the bureaucracy as a professional order, it was necessary not only to include state officials such as judges (administrative officials who stood at the heart of this group), but also clergyman, teachers, and numerous groups of technical officials in public service, such as the post office and the railroads. In addition, there were also local, municipal, and provincial officials with a large army of private officials in the background. Of these groups, Hintze paid special attention to the Catholic clergy, since they could be considered the oldest part of the modern bureaucratic hierarchy and the original model for the secular, political bureaucratic hierarchy.[20] For Hintze, the roots of the bureaucratic order were to be found in the oldest groups that arose out of the mass of the people; that is, in the warrior and clerical orders (358). Although Hintze thought that historically, both public and private bureaucracy stemmed from the same roots, he thought it was best to deal with the core of the bureaucratic order—the public bureaucratic order.

From the time of my doctoral research (1962–67), the three main roots in the development of German and Prussian bureaucracy that Hintze presented in 1911 were of basic importance in almost all of my history classes. In 1967, a summary of these roots became available in English with my summary of this part of Hintze's essay, "Der Beamtenstand" (360–62). In 1968, however, Reinhold Bendix used Hintze's account of the three main roots in the bureaucratization of government in Prussia and Germany as the basis of his classic account of the "Bureaucratization of government" and of the "Development of European bureaucracies" in his article that was simply called, "Bureaucracy." For Bendix, "The term 'bureaucratization' serves to designate this pattern of social change, which can be traced to the royal households of medieval Europe, to the eventual employment of university-trained jurists as administrators, to the civilian transformation

---

19. Ibid., 67.
20. Ibid.

of military controllers on the Continent, and to the civil service reforms in England and the United States in the nineteenth century."[21]

It is significant that while Bendix takes Max Weber and his famous ideal type of "bureaucracy" as his starting point for this six-page article, half of this article is based mainly on Hintze's account of the historical development of bureaucracy in Prussia and Germany. Hintze describes this development from the military retainers in the household of the large lord or prince, to the university trained lawyers and "hired doctors" of the sixteenth century, to the new kind of extraordinary official that appeared in the seventeenth century with the large military state: the commissaries.

For both Hintze and Bendix, the relationship of the official to his lord or ruler was different with each of these three types of office holding. The essential point that Hintze wanted to make about the earliest beginnings of the bureaucracy in Germany was that it went back to the Germanic knightly followers of a large lord and that this original patriarchal spirit or vassal relationship between a lord and his followers had given bureaucracy a stamp that had lasted to the present (360).[22]

This relationship was modified by the appearance at the end of the fifteenth century and during the sixteenth century of the university educated lawyers and humanists, who were the second root in the development of modern bureaucracy in Germany. The new element here was the civil law contract for service that was patterned after Roman contract relationships. There was no patriarchal spirit to be found in this relationship, for here "hired doctors" worked for stipulated wages on a temporary basis. With the employment of university-trained councilors and secretaries, "a new status group developed and was greatly strengthened during the sixteenth century when temporary public service was transformed into life-long employment on a contractual basis."[23] With this change, nobles in Germany found that university training in law was a key to working as an advisor, councilor, or administrator to and for a prince or king. At the same time, they provided much of the leadership in the estates of the German and Prussian provinces. Particularly in Prussia, with the ruler's desire to create a standing army and a large state out of all his provinces, the ruler needed a new kind of official that he appointed and completely controlled for these two purposes.

21. Bendix, "Bureaucracy," 208.
22. Hintze, "Der Beamtenstand," 85.
23. Bendix, "Bureaucracy," 210.

The Expert's Historian

In a brilliant and detailed essay called "The Commissary and His Significance in General Administrative History: A Comparative Study," Hintze discovered a new type of bureaucrat, for to him the concept of the commissariat was a general type under which the Prussian war commissary was an especially important type.[24] The war commissaries in Prussia were specially commissioned agents of the central government whose function was to make sure that "in the mustering of troops, the general, colonel, or captain had filled his quota of men; that the troops were all present and in good order; and that they were receiving the right wages."[25] For Hintze, it was no secret "that the eighteenth century administrative organization derived its characteristic features from the commissarial authorities that had chiefly developed out of the military commissaries."[26] In his essay, "Der Beamtenstand," Hintze clearly identified this "new *commissarischen Beamtentum* as the third important root of the modern *Beamtenstandes.*"[27]

In an important essay that was first presented at the International Conference on Otto Hintze in Berlin in April 1980, and that was called "Otto Hintze, Max Weber, und das Problem der Bürokratie," Jürgen Kocka pointed out that "several years before Max Weber," Hintze had worked out many of the characteristics that Weber had "combined, sharpened, and universalized" into his ideal type "Bureaucracy."[28] Also at this conference, Michael Erbe pointed out that the essay "Der Beamtenstand" became a standard work that was cited over and over,[29] and that while it has been supplemented here and there since it was first published, it certainly has not been refuted.[30]

In 1968, Bendix also wrote a brief account of Hintze's work and significance for the *International Encyclopedia of the Social Sciences*. His evaluation of Hintze's work here is important, for as he concluded: "What remains is a series of essays on administrative history, feudalism, the estate constitutions of Europe, the world-historical conditions of representative

---

24. Hintze, "The Commissary" 281.

25. Ibid., 270.

26. Ibid., 269.

27. Hintze, "Der Beamtenstand," 87.

28. Kocka, "Otto Hintze, Max Weber, und das Problem der Bürokratie," 153.

29. Erbe, "Otto Hintze und seine Sicht der Entstehung des neuzeitlichen Beamtentums," 87.

30. Ibid., 91. Erbe helpfully calls the second part of Hintze's essay "the historical part." Ibid., 88.

institutions in Western European societies, and Polish constitutional history, as well as a brief synopsis of his own views concerning the major phases of European political history. Taken together, these writings do for the study of political institutions what Max Weber's sociology of religion did for the study of religious beliefs. By comparative analysis, they reveal the institutional preconditions that shaped the Western system of constitutional states and the major types of constitutions that emerged within this system."[31]

As Bendix also concluded, "Hintze's work, which is informed with his wide knowledge of history, has a developmental emphasis that is not evolutionist and a conceptual approach that, like Weber's, brings out the singularity of a historical sequence or configuration by means of strategic contrasts with other civilizations." For both Hintze and Weber, "functional relations are the end products of human actions that may produce innovations that are not less genuine because they are conditioned." Also, although Hintze's work "remained fragmentary," Bendix concluded that his work "is a major contribution to the comparative analysis of social and political institutions."[32]

In his excellent and very influential study, *Max Weber, An Intellectual Portrait* in 1960, Reinhard Bendix made a strong and very striking statement about the work of Otto Hintze. Bendix stated: "A continuation of Weber's work as he may have intended it, namely a further application and development of his concepts through comparative analysis, is contained in the work of Otto Hintze." Much of the last chapter of my dissertation in 1967 contains my response to this statement.

Before World War I, sociology was not really recognized as an established academic discipline. After the war, however, German sociology came into its own, and the man who was most responsible for giving this new discipline real academic status was Max Weber (539). One of the interesting but little known facts concerning the establishment of this new discipline in Germany was that for the summer of 1920, Max Weber announced a university course called *"Allgemeine Staatslehre und Politik,"* but when he actually gave the course, the actual title was changed to *"Staatssoziologie"* (540).[33] Thus, one of the disciplines that benefited from the demise of the

---

31. Bendix, "Otto Hintze," 367.
32. Ibid.
33. See Winkelmann, "Introduction," in *Max Weber's Soziologie,* 9.

nineteenth-century discipline called "*Politik*" after World War I, was the discipline called "sociology."

In his essay, called "Der Typus in der Geschichtswissenchaften" in 1958, Theodore Schieder stated that to him, it was astonishing that Hintze was almost the only historian for whom one could trace a direct influence of the historical sociology of Weber and of his theory of types. Schieder found this especially astonishing since this sociology was so deeply rooted in historical ground (540–41).[34]

It is not astonishing, however, that Hintze, more than any other professional historian of his generation, was interested in Weber's work, for they had much in common. First of all, Hintze was the last historian in Germany who gave regular lecture courses on *Politik*. Second, both Hintze and Weber wrote doctoral dissertations that dealt with medieval history. Third, both of them were trained in history, law, and economics. Fourth, both of them became closely associated with the historical school of economics and began their methodological studies with important critiques of the economist and historian, Wilhelm Roscher. Most of all, they shared many common interests. Also, in the case of Hintze, from the beginning, he was searching for basic types of Western historical development.

In the Roscher article of 1897, Hintze said that he was not looking for a clear logical classification of types or for logical types that could be ordered under a unified point of view (517). Instead, he was looking for new, empirical, individual types, which he found in world history since the time of Aristotle. Hintze was interested in historical groups rather than artificial classes, and such groups were to be determined by the entire type of state building, rather than by single characteristics.[35]

Earlier in this essay, Hintze suggested that perhaps Aristotle's three "ideal" or "*ideele Grundformen*" or basic forms of political organization could be traced back to the simple contrast between the "*herrschaftlich*" or authoritative, and the "*genossenschaftlich*" or associative principle of organization, which could be seen in all state building and which had been used very fruitfully and scientifically in recent times.[36]

These two concepts, which remained two favorite connected but polar concepts throughout Hintze's work, were used especially in the famous essay "State Organization and Military Organization." Like the Roscher

---

34. Schieder, "Der Typus in der Geschichtswissenschaft," 177.
35. Hintze, "Roschers politische Entwicklungstheorie," 42.
36. Ibid., 10.

article, this was a forerunner of Hintze's later ideal types on feudalism, *ständische Verfassungen*, and the modern state. It was also, however, a beautiful example of his basic philosophy and view of history.

First of all, this article was an excellent example of how Hintze's comparative studies were based on an application of three cognitive views or analogies—of polar opposites, a catastrophic or dialectic view of development, and an organic view of development. In fact, the entire article was full of opposites: militant and industrial societies; the *herrschaftlich* and the *genossenschaftlich* principles of organization; power and welfare; standing army and militia; rule from above and self government; absolutism and representative institutions; unitary state and federative state; military class and sustaining class; monarchy and republic, etc.

Secondly, Hintze had always found Spencer's famous types, the militant or military and the industrial types of societies,[37] as useful "ideal types" ("*ideele typen*"), which perhaps had never been purely realized in the history of mankind.[38] Hintze, who was the most knowledgeable person in the world on the subject of militant societies at this time, clearly showed how Prussia was "the classic example of the military state" and how "the entire administrative organization there was keyed to military aims and served them," how "every minister of state was also called minister of war," and also how "every councilor in the administrative chamber, every tax councilor, was known also as war councilor."[39]

One of the interests that Weber and Hintze shared was the significance of Calvinism for the development of the modern Western world, and certainly this interest did not stem from Weber. In the year 1902, Hintze pointed to the importance of tendencies stemming from Sweden and the Netherlands, including how Gustavus Adolphus and West European Calvinism provided the impulses that led the electors of Brandenburg to rise out of the misery of the small German principalities and led to the idea of founding a large and powerful state (543). In 1903, a year before *The Protestant Ethic and the Spirit of Capitalism* began to appear, Hintze called attention to the "unending importance" of the conversion of the Hohenzollern to the heroic and dynamic Protestant faith of the Huguenot wars of the Dutch war for independence and of the Puritan revolution. He suggested that, in a certain sense, the entire power politics of the modern monarchy was

---

37. Hintze, "Military Organization," 182.
38. Ibid., 182.
39. Ibid., 201.

born out of West European Calvinism, which the Hohenzollern adopted in contrast to their Lutheran estates (544). In the year 1906, Hintze wrote to Meinecke that the importance of Calvinism went beyond what Weber and Troeltsch had in mind. Hintze suggested that not only capitalism, but also power politics, had its roots in an ascetic view and conduct of life, although Calvinism was not the only thing responsible for this (544).

In emphasizing the importance of the conversion of the Hohenzollern to Calvinism for the whole development of the Prussian state, Hintze was following in the footsteps of his great teacher, Droysen. In 1915, Hintze stated that Reinhold Koser was wrong in entirely rejecting Droysen's interpretation of this subject, since he could not see any heroic activity or power politics in the first two Calvinist rulers of Brandenburg in the seventeenth century (544). Although this view of the connection between Calvinism and power politics was evident in many of Hintze's studies before 1918, it was not until 1931 that he really presented his basic ideas on this subject.

The article "Kalvinismus und Staatsräson in Brandenburg zu Beginn des 17. Jahrhunderts" (1931) was published in the *Historische Zeitschrift* (144:1–47), and it was included in volume 3—*Regierung und Verwaltung: Gesammelte Abhandlungen zur Staats- Rechts- und Sozialgeschichte Prussens* by Gerhard Oestreich in 1967 (255–312). Fortunately, it was also translated into English by Felix Gilbert in 1975. More than any of Hintze's other essays, "it combines his [Hintze's] early concern with Brandenburg-Prussian history, and his more recent interest in sociology and in the questions Weber and Troeltsch had raised about the influence of Protestantism on the development of the modern world."[40] This essay is very important for a number of reasons, for as Gilbert also stated, it includes "insights that illuminate the entire institutional development in modern Europe."[41]

Years before Gilbert translated this article, I found powerful insights for all of my work as a history teacher when I discovered a page-long translated passage from this essay in Reinhard Bendix's classic study *Max Weber: An Intellectual Portrait*,[42] which dealt with Marx's powerful "substructure/superstructure" image. I had first emphasized this page in my dissertation in 1967 (546–47) as part of my discussion of the work of Weber and Hintze,

---

40. Hintze, "Calvinism and Raison d'Etat," 88. There is one obvious mistake in Gilbert's translation on p. 93, line 6, where he uses the words "by capitalism" when he clearly means by or through "Calvinism" in stating Hintze's hypothesis.

41. Ibid., 89.

42. Bendix, *Max Weber*, 69.

but from 1969 to my retirement in 1998, I used the following translations as a handout every year at the end of my discussion of Marx's "substructure/superstructure" image when we were dealing with *The Communist Manifesto* in our "World Civilizations" course.

In my study *Religion and the Rise of History* in 2009, I emphasized how, like Ranke, both Hintze and Weber believed that "idealism" and "self-interest" were basic forces in life and history. More than Weber, however, Hintze was able to articulate an "at-the-same-time image" that not only characterized the way they approached the study of religion and society, but also supplemented and demystified Ranke's idealistic view of the state as a *"real-geistige,"* or an "earthly-spiritual community."[43]

As Reinhard Bendix made clear to all of his readers in the year 1960, "Yet nowhere in Weber's work did he clearly articulate a view of 'the relative independence and intricate interdependence of ideas and economic interests' that guided his work.[44] Fortunately," Bendix said, "such a formulation could be found in the work of Otto Hintze":[45]

> All human action arises from a common source, in political as well as in religious life. Everywhere, the first impulse to social action is given as a rule by real interests, i.e., by political and economic interests. But idea interests lend wings to these real interests, give them a spiritual mean, and serve to justify them. Man does not live by bread alone. He wants to have a good conscience as he pursues his life-interests. And in pursuing them, he develops his capacities to the highest extent only if he believes that in so doing he serves a higher, rather than a purely egoistic purpose. Interests without such "spiritual wings" are lame, but on the other hand, ideas can win out in history only if and insofar as they are also associated with real interests.[46]

For Hintze, the Marxian image of substructure and superstructure did not give "adequate expression to this peculiar connection of interests and ideas," for in this image "ideologies: quickly lose all reality." Moreover, the Marxian model had "the flaw that it is static despite the fact that it seeks to portray a dynamic transformation [of society]. Where a substructure is transformed, the superstructure does not follow suit by transforming itself

---

43. Smith, *Religion and the Rise of History*, 235.
44. Bendix, *Max Weber*, 68.
45. Ibid., 68–69.
46. Ibid., 69.

in corresponding fashion. Rather, the superstructure disintegrates along with the whole of society."[47]

At this point, Hintze and Bendix presented Hintze's at-the-same-time image that supplemented not only the life work of Leopold von Ranke, but also of the work of Max Weber, Hintze's greatest contemporary and kindred spirit for understanding Western social historical thought. "I think," Hintze said,

> A more appropriate image is that of a polar coordination of interests and ideas. In the long run, neither of the two can survive without the other, historically speaking; each requires the other as supplementation. *Wherever interests are vigorously pursued, an ideology tends to be developed also to give meaning, re-enforcement and justification to these interests. And this ideology is an indispensable part of the life-process, which is expressed in action. Conversely, wherever ideas are to conquer the world, they require the leverage of real interests, although frequently ideas will more or less detract these interests from their original aim* . . .[48]

In these words, as I claimed in *Religion and the Rise of History*, "Hintze provided his generation and generations of scholars and teachers since his time with an 'at-the-same-time' and an unsurpassed image to augment the powerful Marxist and materialist "substructure /superstructure image."[49] And, for me personally, these pages from *Max Weber: An Intellectual Portrait*, were the greatest contribution of Reinhard Bendix to Hintze studies during the twentieth century.

From 1922 to 1927, Hintze wrote three book reviews dealing with the work of Max Weber, and in 1964, Gerhard Oestreich included all three reviews in *Soziologie und Geschichte*, volume two of Hintze's *Gesammelte Abhandlungen zur Soziologie, Politik, und Geschichte*. The first of these reviews (1922), "Max Webers Religionssoziologie," was a review of the three volumes of Weber's collected articles dealing with "Religionssoziologie" that were published in 1920–21. Here, Hintze emphasized how Weber's "epoch-making" *The Protestant Ethic and the Spirit of Capitalism* was not only the

---

47. Ibid.

48. Ibid., Here the italics are provided by Bendix, and they are neither in the original nor in the translation of this article by Gilbert in *The Historical Essays of Otto Hintze*, 94–95.

49. Smith, *Religion and the Rise of History*, 237.

high point of this collection, but also despite its many critics, should be considered "as certain academic truth."[50]

In 1926, Hintze published a review that was titled "Max Weber's Sociology"—a review of Weber's posthumously published work with the title *Economy and Society*. Despite the title, Hintze said, this work could also be called a "System of Sociology."[51] The fact that part of this work was written in the years 1911–1913 and still did not seem dated to Hintze in 1926, despite the enormous changes in values with World War I, was—as Hintze pointed out—a splendid testimony to Weber's objectivity.[52]

One of the most important points that Hintze made both about Max Weber's famous ideal-type methodology and his sociology as a whole, was that they were "nominalistic." Weber's approach was nominalistic, he said, for his method involved using so-called "ideal types" instead of the usual concepts of the natural sciences. These ideal types were used to grasp the meaning of historical-social reality in firm thought forms. He didn't say what matter is, but rather, what he would name it. Thus, he defined names and not things. For Hintze, Weber's "definition," with all its conceptual sharpness, was always and at the same time *"anschaulich beschreibend"* or perceivable and descriptive (552).[53]

Three of the splendid discoveries of Weber's sociology that Hintze greatly praised were his three types of *Herrschaft*—rational, traditional, and charismatic—for they were enormously enlightening for both history and the social sciences. No less epoch making for Hintze was Weber's use of these "wonder lamps" to explore the social and political structures of the most important civilizations of world history, including the Christian occident.[54]

One of Hintze's main points about Weber's sociology was that the *herrschaftlich*, or the authoritative direction and government, far outweighed the *genossenschaftlich*, or the associative aspect of political and social life, for *"genossenschaftlich* solidarity" was stressed very weakly.[55]

---

50. Hintze, "Max Webers Religionssoziologie," 129.
51. Hintze, "Max Webers Soziologie," 135.
52. Ibid., 137.
53. Ibid., 140. The date 1925 on p. 552 of "Otto Hintze's Comparative Constitutional History of the West" should be 1926, the date for this review.
54. Ibid., 143–44.
55. Ibid., 142.

The democracy that Weber envisioned was above all, leader democracy ("*Führerdemokratie*").[56]

Another main point that Hintze emphasized was that for Weber, the category of development played a very subordinate role in his work. Hintze realized that this was important for his clear, systematic approach, and also so that sociology would not dissolve into history. However, this meant that dynamic relationships would never come to full justice.[57]

Although Hintze praised Weber's discussion of the concept of feudalism, he thought that this concept also needed to include non-western areas, for to Hintze, feudalism was not uniquely Western. For Hintze, the only uniquely Western kinds of constitutions were the *ständische* or estates constitutions, and to him, these constitutions arose out of the unique relationship between *Sacerdotium* and *Imperium*, which was both basic and formative to the Christian Occident and to the rise of the European state system.[58]

In this review, Weber also emphasized that the comparative method in the hand of the Historian led more to sharper differentiation and mutual separation of the real, individual type, while the ideal types of the sociologist are only for structural analysis and not to be used for the synthetic formation of connected groups of phenomenon.[59] Both for sociological research and for purely historical research, for Hintze, this was an "epoch-making work."[60]

The most important sentence for me in this review, however, was "that this sociology cries out for a constitutional-historical supplement."[61] This important sentence was cited by Gerhard Oestreich in his very important essay, "Otto Hintze's Stellung zur Politik." For me, this statement also meant that the life work of a comparative constitutional history of the West that Hintze set out to accomplish as a needed supplement to the life work of Leopold von Ranke, could also serve as a needed supplement to the life work of his great contemporary, Max Weber. This was a main theme of my dissertation in 1967, and was also the main theme of my study, *Religion and the Rise of History* in 2009.

56. Ibid., 143.
57. Ibid., 144.
58. Ibid., 146–47.
59. Ibid., 146.
60. Ibid., 147.
61. Ibid., 144.

Otto Hintze and Max Weber

In 1927, Hintze published a very favorable, sensitive, and seven-page review of Marianne Weber's large (712 pages) biography of her husband, *Max Weber, Ein Lebensbild*. Here, Hintze pointed out that when Max Weber died, there was some embarrassment concerning what philosophical discipline to use for him, for he was a jurist, a historian, and a national economist. For Hintze, however, all of these roles did not cover his scholarly activities. While Jaspers proclaimed that Weber was a philosopher, Rickert disagreed with this, and even Weber declined this designation. For Hintze, however, in some respects this designation was correct.[62] Most of all, it was clear to Hintze that no one in Germany had done more to raise sociology to the rank of a real academic discipline than Max Weber.[63]

One of the things that tied Hintze and Weber together is that both of them were universal scholars. As Gerhard Oestreich emphasized, Hintze was universal in a double sense. From an early time, he was a universal *historian,* for as the Roscher article of 1897 showed, he felt at home in all ages and presented his own views. Also, at an early time, he was a universal *scholar* in that he sought to combine and bring together the conceptual and opposing languages of history, political science, law, economics, and social theory. Here, Oestreich was also right when he claimed that this is what made it possible for him to allow the sociology of Max Weber, Franz Oppenheimer, and Werner Sombart to come into their own right.[64]

Today, one can also agree with Gerhard Oestreich's view that the real assessment or appreciation of Hintze's life work lies in Hintze's great comparative constitutional researches of the second half of the 1920s. However, one does not need to agree to the second part of this sentence where Oestreich argues that these great studies "could not have been written without the methodological and subject matter stimulus of Max Weber's work." While this may or may not be true, it is not something that can be proven. In my dissertation, I tried to summarize and evaluate all of Hintze's writings from this period of his life, but here, I can only emphasize the significance of his discovery of historical ideal types from 1926 to 1932.

One of the most important facts that I learned in 1964 when I was doing research in the Archive der Deutschen Akademie der Wissenschaften zu Berlin, was that on January 26, 1926, Hintze presented a lecture to the Academy called "Typologie der ständischen Verfassungen des

---

62. Hintze, review of Marianne Weber, *Max Weber: Ein Lebensbild*, 150.
63. Ibid., 151.
64. Oestreich, "Otto Hintze's Stellung zur Politikwissenschaft und Soziologie," 26.

Abendlandes" (71). At this time, I also learned that on March 27, 1927, this typology was followed by a lecture to the Academy concerning "Die allgemeinen historischen Bedingungen für die Ausbildung ständischer Verfassungen im Christlichen Abendlande" (71). In my dissertation, I confidently asserted: "These two studies, the first of which was published in 1930 and the second in 1931, were the high point of Hintze's study of the development of representative institutions in the West" (71–72).

Today, I am still certain that the first of these two lectures was the basis of Hintze's published ideal type with the same title in 1930. I also believe that the second one also provided a starting point for the essay that was later called "Weltgeschichtliche Bedingungen der Repräsentivverfassung" and that was translated into English in 1975 as "The Preconditions of Representative Government in the Context of World History." Today, as I was both in 1967 and in my study *Religion and the Rise of History* in 2009, I am still convinced that a careful examination of the structure of Hintze's three ideal types demonstrates that the essay called "Typologie der ständische Verfassungen des Abendlandes" is the one that was written first and is therefore the oldest of his three historical ideal types.

At the beginning of his ideal type called "Typologie der ständische Verfassungen des Abendlandes," Hintze pointed out that a comparative consideration of the *ständische* corporate constitutions of Europe had never been seriously considered either in or outside Germany. For Hintze, this certainly was a necessity, for the ständische constitutions were the preliminary stage of the modern representative constitutions, which were unique to the Christian Occident, and which could not be found in the other great cultures of world history (523). Since this title was the same as the ideal type that was first published in 1930, and since Hintze's first published ideal type—"The Nature and Transformation of Feudalism"[65]—was first published in 1929, a question that Hintze scholars have to face is "What was Hintze's first and oldest ideal type?"

In March 1920, Hintze's request for release from his duties at the University of Berlin because of bad health was officially granted. Hintze still hoped to accomplish the main life goals that he had first announced in the Roscher article of 1897, as he made clear in a letter to Meinecke on August 30, 1921 (67–68), but at that time, he viewed his goals from a considerably different perspective and attitude than they had originally been conceived (68). In the comparative studies that Hintze wrote after 1920, Hintze was

---

65. Hintze, "Wesen und Verbreitung des Feudalismus."

even more interested in investigating the development of representative institutions in the West, and this became increasingly apparent in the papers that he presented to the Prussian Academy of Sciences (70–1)—the real center of Hintze's activities from 1921 outside of his own academic household (69).[66]

---

66. For an introduction to Hedwig Hintze's "teas" for her husband in the 1920s, see my footnote number 188 on page 69 of my dissertation, and especially Gerhard, "Otto Hintze—Persönlichkeit und Werk," 3–7 and 9.

4

Frederick C. Beiser and *The German Historicist Tradition*

A Critical Review by Leonard S. Smith

FREDERICK C. BEISER'S *THE German Historicist Tradition* (Oxford: Oxford University Press, 2011) is a masterful work that should be read by every historian and philosopher who has used and admired R. G. Collingwood's *The Idea of History*. Collingwood's book is still helpful for understanding classical and Christian historiography and especially for understanding the first great transition in Western historical thought at the time of St. Augustine (354–430). The book is much less helpful though for understanding modern historical thought and the transition to a distinctly modern historical consciousness, especially in Germany from the 1750s to the founding of the University of Berlin in the year 1810. One reason for this is that Collingwood had little appreciation for what Beiser calls "The German Historicist Tradition." Thus, for understanding the idea of history as a whole, Beiser's book is a necessary supplement to Collingwood.

Every historian and philosopher should read Beiser's recent book, for it is a needed supplement to Ernst Troelstch (1865–1923) and his large study called *Der Historismus und seine Probleme* (1922), as well as to Friedrich Meinecke (1862–1954) and his classic study from the year 1936, *Die Entstehung des Historismus*.

Before Troeltsch became a professor of philosophy at the University of Berlin in 1915 and a colleague and close friend of Friedrich Meinecke, the term *"Historismus"* was not a common term in German historical thought; and when it was used, it usually had negative connotations. At Berlin, however, Troeltsch strenuously sought to make the term *"Historismus"* a positive one by disconnecting it from its negative connotations; for to him "it was the problem of the *significance and nature of historicism itself,* whereby this word is to be completely disconnected from its bad secondary meaning and to be understood in the sense of the basic historizing of all our thought about man, his culture, and his values."[1]

It was important for the idea of history (1) that Meinecke published several articles in the *Historische Zeitschrift* that in 1922 became the basis of *Der Historismus und seine Probleme,* and (2) that he also adopted the term *"Historismus"* from Troeltsch. In 1924, this term became a basic one in Meinecke's second large intellectual history, *Die Idee der Staatsräson,* for here, he emphasized how around the beginning of the nineteenth century, an intellectual revolution took place in Germany. To Meinecke, this revolution was perhaps the greatest revolution in thought experienced by the West, and he associated it with the terms "idealism" and "historicism."[2] Most of all, Meinecke—more than anyone else—made the term "historicism" a basic one for German and Western historical thought, especially with his history called *Die Entstehung des Historismus* (1936).

In his preliminary remarks to his work, Meineke explained how "historicism" was "nothing but the application to the historical world of the new life principles achieved by the great German movement from Leibniz to the death of Goethe." For Meinecke, the essence of historicism was "the substitution of a process of *individualizing* observation for a *generalizing* view of human forces in history." This did not mean "that the historical method excludes altogether any attempt to find general laws in human life," he said, but it had "to make use of this approach and blend it with a feeling for the individual." For Meinecke, the sense of individuality was something new that historicism created.[3]

In his masterful treatment of German philosophy in the year 1987 titled *The Fate of Reason: German Philosophy from Kant to Fichte,* Frederick C. Beiser discussed the work of Hamann, Herder, Kant, and others without mentioning these books by Troeltsch and Meinecke or the significance of the term "historicism" for the late eighteenth century. However, since the

---

1. Troeltsch, *Der Historismus und seine Probleme,* 102.
2. Meinecke, *Machiavellism,* 362.
3. Meinecke, *Historism:* iv.

year 1992, and the appearance of the book *Enlightenment, Revolution, and Romanticism: The Genesis of Modern German Political Thought, 1790–1800*, the term "*Historismus*" has been of basic importance for Beiser. Indeed, here he argues that "the most potent threat to the *Aufklärung* in the 1790's came ... from the rise of historicism."[4] Here, he also provided his understanding of the main characteristics of historicism.

"Reduced to its bare essentials," Beiser claimed, "it consists of three central theses. First, all social, political, and cultural institutions and activities are subject to change and adapted to their circumstances, so that there is no single ideal constitution, language, religion, or culture."[5] Second, a culture is a "nonrecurring, unique whole, an organic unity or individual, whose beliefs, institutions, traditions, and language are all inseparable from one another."[6] Third, according to Beiser, "the development of every culture is organic, showing the stages of growth of any living being: birth, youth, decay, and death. All of these can be seen as a consequence of applying an organic metaphor to society."[7]

Although neither Meinecke's nor Troeltsch's names appear in the index for this book, in note six of his "Introduction," Beiser states: "The classic treatment of the origins of historicism in Germany is Friedrich Meinecke, *Die Entstehung des Historismus*." Further, in note eight, he quotes Meinecke's statement (in German) that "historicism was nothing else than the application of new life principles to historical life."[8] In the rest of the book, however, Beiser cites Meinecke only twice[9] and does not mention Troeltsch and his definition of historicism at all.

In a chapter called "Hegel's historicism" (1993) in *The Cambridge Companion to Hegel*, which Beiser edited, he provides a brief reference to Meinecke, and he also offers a very brief definition of the term "historicism." First of all, Beiser claims that "Hegel's historicism amounted to nothing less than a revolution in the history of philosophy."[10] In reference

---

4. Beiser, *Enlightenment, Revolution, and Romanticism*, 5.
5. Ibid.
6. Ibid., 6.
7. Ibid.
8. Ibid., 367; Meinecke, Die *Enstehung des Historismus*, 2.

9. Note 2, p. 395 and note 113, p. 400. In 2002, Harvard University Press published a book by Frederick C. Beiser called *German Idealism: The Struggle against Subjectivism, 1781–1801*. Here, there is no mention of Meinecke or Troeltsch, and the term "historicism" is only mentioned in the preface.

10. Beiser, "Hegel's Historicism," 270.

to Meinecke, Beiser simply states: "The definitive study of the origins of historicism is Friedrich Meinecke (Munich 1959). Unfortunately, Meinecke does not discuss Hegel."[11] Here, Beiser explains that "If Hegel's historicism amounted to a revolution, it still was not a radical break with the past. For historicism, understood in a broad sense as the doctrine that emphasizes the importance of history for the understanding of human institutions and activities, must by definition also be the product of history."[12]

As Beiser claims in his opening paragraph: "History cannot be assigned to a corner of Hegel's system, relegated to a few paragraphs near the end of the *Encyclopedia,* or confined to his *Lectures on the Philosophy of History*. For as many scholars have long since recognized, history is central to Hegel's concept of philosophy. One of the most striking characteristics of Hegel's thought is that it *historicizes* philosophy, explaining its purposes, principles, and problems in historical terms."[13] The word "historizing" was made famous mainly by Ernst Troeltsch, just as his Heidelberg friend, Max Weber, had popularized the phrase "the rationalizing" of all aspects of life.

In the year 2007, Frederick Beiser plunged fully into the problems, meaning, and history of historicism in an important chapter in *The Oxford Handbook of Continental Philosophy*. This chapter was simply called "Historicism." One of the reasons that this essay is important for historians is because here, an outstanding authority on the late Enlightenment in Germany strongly agreed with Meinecke by stating: "The historical significance of historicism is best measured by its *break* with the Enlightenment, which had dominated European intellectual life during the eighteenth century."[14] More than that, Beiser strongly defended Meinecke against those contemporary historians who "rejected Meinecke's paradigm as simplistic and misleading"; who "advocated seeing a continuum rather than a break between historicism and the Enlightenment"; and who "criticized Meinecke for making a point he would never have questioned." Beiser indeed went to great pains to demonstrate that historicism had its roots in the historiography of the Enlightenment.[15]

While Beiser's interaction with Meinecke and his last great intellectual history is one of the main things to note about this essay, the most important

11. Ibid., note 3, 298.
12. Ibid., 271.
13. Ibid., 270.
14. Beiser, "Historicism," 164.
15. Ibid., 165.

aspect is that here, he provides an introduction to "the German historicist tradition" from its beginning to the early twentieth century and to the work that appeared four years later (2011): *The German Historicist Tradition*. Thus, this essay shows how Beiser was vastly extending his knowledge and expertise on German historical thought, beginning with "the founders" J. A. Chladenius (1710–59) and Christoph Gatterer (1727–1799)" and "the godfathers" Johann Georg Hamann (1744–1803), Johann Gottfried Herder (1744–1803), Wilhelm von Humboldt (1767–1835), and Justus Möser (1720–1794). Also included in his list of historicists, were the leading historians of the nineteenth century, or "the proper age of historicism"— Barthold Georg Niebuhr (1775–1831), Leopold von Ranke (1795–1886), Johann Gustav Droysen (1838–84), and Jacob Burckhardt (1818–1897)— plus "the founders" of the historical school of law; that is, Friedrich Savigny (1799–1761) and Karl Friedrich Eichhorn (1781–1854).[16]

Another reason this essay marks a change for Beiser from his earlier works is that here, he emphasizes how "the historicist agenda" was to make history a science. With this new emphasis, both here and in *The German Historicist Tradition*, he departs from the view of historicism of Troeltsch and Meinecke because for them, historicism was basically a way of viewing life based on the principles of individuality and development. The importance of this change is especially reflected in where Beiser begins his story. Indeed, unlike Meinecke, Beiser begins his story with J. A. Chladenius and the idea of a *Geschichtswisssenschaft* or historical science. This new emphasis, more than anything else, signified that for Beiser, the term "historicist tradition" includes more than what Troeltsch and Meinecke meant by the term "historicism."

One of the ways that Beiser enlarges our knowledge of the origins of modern historical thought is through this emphasis, including through his magnificent thirty-page treatment of Chladenius in his chapter called "Chladenius and the New Science of History," and through his opening and closing statements. Indeed, Beiser opened his study with the statement that "The history of historicism should begin with Johann Martin Chladenius (1710–59)" (27), and closed with the conclusion that "We can see "Chladenius's *Allgemeine Geschichtswissenschaft* as the founding document of the historicist tradition" (62).

---

16. Ibid., 156–57. Of this list of historicists, Beiser chose not to have a separate chapter on Christoph Gatterer.

In chapter 2, titled "Justus Möser and the Roots of Historicism," Beiser demonstrates a masterful understanding of Möser as a historian and also describes Meinecke's treatment of him in *Die Enstehung des Historismus*. Like Meinecke, Beiser sees Möser as a father of historicism and as a champion of the principle of individuality, but here, he claims that "What makes Möser the father of historicism is precisely his recognition of the importance of rootedness, attachment, and belonging" (66). Moreover, for Beiser, "These would become fundamental values for the whole historicist tradition; but their first formulation appears clearly in Möser, who spearheaded its reaction against modernity." It was these values, Beiser argues, "that are behind Möser's adoption of one fundamental and characteristic theme of historicism: the principle of individuality" (66).

In chapter 3, "Herder's Historicism, its Genesis and Development," Beiser not only builds on his previous intensive studies of Herder, but also attempts "to fill in the gaps" in the "masterful" but "remarkably patchy and incomplete" story that Meinecke told. "Already in the 1760s," Beiser claims, "the young Herder had completely historicized philosophy" (105). One of the many aspects to admire about Beiser's treatment of Herder and the origins of historicism that far surpasses Meinecke, was the significance of theology for Herder. Although Beiser shows how Herder's "anthropology gave birth to his principle of development," and "his aesthetics gave rise to his principle of individuality" around "the middle of the eighteenth century in Germany," he argues that "there arose a new direction of theology that would have the greatest importance for Herder's historical thought. This was the historical school of Biblical interpretation" (110).

This chapter and each of the first eight chapters of Beiser's *The German Historicist Tradition* are indispensable reading for all professional historians who teach courses in historiography and who attempt to cover what Collingwood called "The Idea of History." Chapter 4 deals with "Humboldt the Proteus"; chapter 5 with "Savigny and the Historical School of Law"; chapter 6 with "Ranke's Romantic Philosophy"; chapter 7 with "The Historics of Johann Gustav Droysen"; and chapter 8 with "Dilthey and the Foundations of the Human Sciences." In each of these chapters and in these first 364 pages as a whole, Beiser demonstrates a command of his subjects, a depth of knowledge, and a knowledge of the literature on each of his subjects that is both remarkable and very useful for historians.

One of the few places that I would disagree with Beiser in these chapters is in chapter 4 on Humboldt, where Beiser said that Meinecke "traces the principle of individuality back to Ranke" (168). Like Meinecke, however, Beiser also traces this principle back to Möser (p. 66) and Herder (106–7).

In his excellent chapter on Ranke, there are two places where Beiser's statements are too strong. First, the statement, "Ranke's skepticism about world history would abate somewhat in his later years" (265), is too strong both for Ranke's work as a whole and especially for his final years when he was dictating volume after volume of his unfinished world history. In fact, I don't know of any time in his life when Ranke did not believe that world history was not the highest kind of history.

Second is the statement, "The aim of the Rankean historian, however, is basically *intuitive*, lying outside the realm of intellectual discourse entirely" (265). While the first part of this statement is true of some historians who would call themselves "Rankean," I doubt that any German historian who believes, like Ranke, that history is a *Wissenschaft*, would accept the second part of this sentence."

Additionally, this use of the term "intuitive," does not apply to the greatest successor of Ranke in the twentieth century—Otto Hintze (1861–1940). For the best discussion of this question by a professional historian of Meinecke's and Hintze's generation, see Hintze's very important review of Georg Simmel's *Die Probleme der Geschichtsphilosophie* (2nd edition, 1905) in *Schmoller's Jahrbuch*, 30 (1906) 809–14. For "Anglophone readers," (a term used in this work [vii]), a nine-page summary of this review can be found in my unpublished dissertation, "Otto Hintze's Comparative Constitutional History of the West" (St. Louis: Washington University, 1967), 460–69.

Another place where I would question a Beiser statement on Ranke, is where he writes, "insofar as he claims that the subject matter of history is the individual." Here, I think that both Troeltsch and Hintze were right when they emphasized that what historians, such as Ranke, basically dealt with were individual totalities and units of life (*Lebensheiten*), as I discuss below.

The last five chapters of this book are also very important, but here, professional historians might have some problems, for these chapters would appeal mainly to philosophers. Chapter 9 deals with "Wilhelm Windelband and the Forces of History"; chapter 10 deals with "Rickert and the Philosophy of Value"; chapter 11 deals with "Emil Lask and the End of Southwestern Neo-Kantianism"; chapter 12 deals with "Simmel's Early Historicism"; and chapter 13 deals with "Max Weber and the end of the Historicist

Tradition." The first problem that historians would have with these chapters is that Beiser doesn't include any twentieth-century German historians. Secondly, he doesn't include either Troeltsch or Meinecke—the two most important individuals for the discovery and use of the term "historicism" as a positive term for scholars to use. Thirdly, he doesn't include Otto Hintze, who was not only the most universal and Rankean professional historian of his generation, but who most personified Humboldt's ideal historian; that is, a *philosophical historian* (191). Therefore, it is difficult for historians to agree with Beiser that "Rickert, Lask, Simmel, and Weber were the main historicists of the early twentieth century" (365). This might be true within the field of philosophy, since the Neo-Kantians "wanted philosophy to be an independent science as much as the historicists wanted history to be so" (365), but this is certainly a change of emphasis in this book.

Beiser is correct, however, when he points out that the "Neo Kantian attitude toward historicism was highly ambivalent," for "while on the one hand, they attempted to aid historicism and to provide history with a secure foundation" (366), on the other hand, the neo-Kantians viewed history as a threat that had to be contained. For history, like all disciplines, had a tendency toward not only autonomy, but hegemony" (366).

In these last chapters and with this emphasis on philosophy as a science, historians will find the reading less familiar and more analytical than the earlier chapters. This is less so for the last chapter, "Max Weber and the End of Historicism." Indeed, this chapter should be read by all historians, philosophers, sociologists, and social scientists, for it relates to all of these areas. One of the sections of this chapter that should interest scholars in all areas is Beiser's very sophisticated and helpful discussion of Weber's "Ideal Types" (544–50).

Most of all, however, historians can and should question Beiser's opening statement to his excellent chapter on Max Weber: "The historicist tradition in Germany reached its culmination, and came to a close in the work of Max Weber (1864–1920)" (511). One of the main problems both with this statement and with this book as a whole is that it leaves out the brilliant essay by Otto Hintze that was published by Friedrich Meinecke in the *Historische Zeitschrift* in the year 1927—an essay that was called "Ernst Troeltsch and the Problems of Historicism: Critical Studies," and that has been translated into English in *The Historical Essays of Otto Hintze* (1975). Related to this problem, is the fact that Beiser was not aware of my study, *Religion and the Rise of History: Martin Luther and the Cultural Revolution in Germany, 1760–1810*, which was published in April, 2009 and includes the story of the debate between Hintze and Meinecke from 1888 through Meinecke's *Die Entstehung des Historismus* in 1936—a debate that Troeltsch participated in from 1915 to his death in 1923.

In my study *Religion and the Rise of History*, readers will find both a historical typology of Western historical thought from the time of Herodotus through the work of Troeltsch, Meinecke, and Hintze and a discussion of their great debate focusing on the nature of historicism. Here, I can just present my translation of Hintze's often ignored but brilliant definition of historicism—a definition that has to be included within the story of the history of historicism or that story is not complete. Before doing this, however, I need to make just a few additional points that Hintze made in this essay.

One of the main problems that Hintze found with Troeltsch's *Der Historismus und seine Probleme* was that Troeltsch had not made a sharp distinction between historicism as a methodology and as a *Weltanschauung*. For Troeltsch, Hintze argued, the general philosophical function of historicism—which was to provide the materials for both a cultural synthesis and the historical process—took precedence over the purely epistemological function. Therefore, in "interests of a clear methodology," he said, he preferred to see historicism as "nothing more than another mode of thought, another set of methodological categories."[17]

While Hintze also criticized Troeltsch "for having no interest whatsoever in psychological methods, he credited him for discussing "the two concepts fundamental to specifically historical thought: the concept of individuality and that of development."[18] Before Hintze explained how these two concepts were based on two simple analogies that historians use in constituting historical objects, however, he said that in his view, the only decisive criterion for determining an object of historical study is "its comprehensibility as a life-unit [*Lebenseinheit*]."

Troeltsch had used the term "*Lebenseinheit*" and had discussed the significance of "individual totalities" in *Der Historimus* volume, but the way Hintze used these terms and connected them with his definition of historicism was distinctive: "What we call historicism is a new, categorical-structure of the mind [Geistes] that began to arise in the eighteenth century and achieved authoritative currency in the nineteenth century, though not in Germany alone. It is characterized by the categories of individuality and

---

17. Hintze, "Troeltsch and the Problems of Historicism," 373.
18. Ibid., 381.

development, which postulate a view of historical reality based on the analogy of the life-unit [*Lebenseinheit*] and the life-process [*Lebensprozess*]."[19]

In the year 1964, Calvin G. Rand wrote an article that was based on Hintze's distinction between historicism as a methodology and as a *Weltanschauung* and that was called "Two Meanings of Historicism in the Writings of Dilthey, Troeltsch, and Meinecke." Although Hintze is credited for this distinction in one footnote[20] and is not mentioned in the text, this article has stuck in my memory for almost fifty years. It did so primarily for two reasons. First of all, for Rand, historicism as a general methodology and as a *Weltanschauung* were "based upon the concepts of individuality, development, and relatedness."[21] From the time that I first read this essay, I rejected the term "relatedness" as a basic concept for historicism as a methodology, for it destroyed the classic simplicity of Hintze's two basic concepts for doing history—the concepts of individuality and development.

Secondly, I have never forgotten the last lines of this essay: "Thus it appears best to regard historicism more formally and only as a broad methodology. The relevance for the mid-twentieth century is another question. But if it is judged relevant by historians and philosophers, it will more than likely be done so on the basis of its methodological value."[22]

In his "Introduction" to *The German Historicist Tradition*, Beiser makes a statement that most of the historicists that he deals with would regard as too strong: "The historicist holds, therefore, that the *essence, identity or nature* of everything in the human world is made by history, so that it is *entirely* the product of the particular historical process that brought it into being." What most historicists would disagree with is the word "*entirely,*" for this would go both against their religious beliefs and what they could actually know.

One of the main differences between Beiser's early treatments and definitions of historicism and those in this book was within what he called "the defining principles of historicism." In his earlier work—like Troeltsch, Meinecke, and Hintze—he emphasized the concepts of individuality and development. In *The German Historicist Tradition*, however, he has

19. Smith, *Religion and the Rise of History*, 242. This translation is close to Gilbert's translation in *The Historical Essays of Otto Hintze*, 390, and also to my earlier translation (1967) in "Otto Hintze's Comparative Constitutional History of the West," 493–94.

20. Rand, "Two Meanings of Historicism," 13.

21. Ibid., 507 and 517. In this article, however, Rand did not say where he got the term "relatedness" or how it could be a methodological concept.

22. Ibid., 518.

substituted the term "holism" for the word "development." This change, however, makes it impossible to see historicism as an at-the-same-time methodology in the way that Hintze did, wherein every human object is seen both as an "historical individuality" and as an "historical process" based on the Kantian concepts of space and time.

Just as Calvin Rand ruined the classic simplicity of Hintze's definition of historicism as a method for doing history when he added the term "relatedness," so Beiser has rejected the classic case for history as a methodology by substituting the word "holism" for Ranke's, Troeltsch's, Meineke's, and Hintze's two basic concepts for modern historical thought: the concepts of individuality and development. Thus the two main problems with Beiser's very impressive work are (1) his failure to discuss Hintze's brilliant, analytical, and philosophical essay called "Troeltsch and the Problems of Historicism: Critical Studies," with its definition of historicism, and (2) the changing of one of the two main words that modern historians have used since the time of Herder to one that they seldom use.

When Hintze wrote his definition of historicism, he wrote it for the purposes of making it a useful term for historians for doing history and for making it an inclusive term that could be used by Marxists and Positivists and scholars from all countries. Thus for him, historicism was not a term that was limited in time. Most of all, as a method of inquiry, historicism would not be a thing of the past, but a useful set of categories for future scholars to use.

Today, there is a great need for historians and philosophers to examine Hintze's essay "Troeltsch and the Problems of Historcism: Critical Studies" and his definition of historicism as a methodology. Today, there is no better-qualified philosopher to do this than Frederick C. Beiser. Today, there is also a need for a book like H. Stuart Hughes, *Consciousness and Society: The Reorientation of European Thought, 1890–1930*, but that includes English and American scholars and both Max Weber and Otto Hintze. There is no one I know who would be more qualified to write a book like this than the author of *The German Historicist Tradition*.

Appendix
Inaugural Speech of Mr. Hintze

WHEN THE ROYAL ACADEMY of Science honored me by accepting me as one of your members, it was probably guided by the view that since I have participated many years in working on the Acta Borussica and last year, through your trust, was called to the commission in charge of the direction of this publication, that also in the future I would be in a position to give you profitable service in this great work. I hope to be able to accomplish this expectation all the more since the studies connected with that publication have been the center of my scientific interests for a long time.

Prepared through historical-philological and legal-political science studies and finally influenced especially by the vigorous interpretation of administrative and economic history as represented by Gustav Schmoller, in 1888, I placed myself in the service of Acta Borussica. First of all, I worked on the history of the establishment of the silk industry, through Frederick the Great, as a typical example of mercantilist trade politics. For this, there was an abundance of material, in part gathered by Schmoller. Then, I worked on the records pertaining to the organization of government and the functioning of the internal administration of the Prussian State from the beginning of the reign of Frederick II until the Seven Year's War. This was a publication that included the new manifestations of enlightened absolutism, especially the administrative organization of the newly acquired provinces, the far-reaching legal reforms of "Grosskanzler" Cocceji, the renewed instruction for the general directory and the provincial chambers, and leads up to a peak in the inclusive statement of the principles of government of the Great King given in his Political Testament of 1752. In an introductory volume, I endeavored in a penetrating survey to analyze the constitution and administration of the Prussian state around

APPENDIX

the year 1740. I came to the conclusion that the distinction of the regional (*landschaftlich*)—territorial and of the great state type in organs and institutions—provided a particularly helpful point of departure that previously hardly had been made use of. This distinction leads immediately into the core of the problem of the origin of absolutism and its creation—the modern and militaristic great state.

In connection with these studies—partly as a prerequisite for them, partly as a result—I had to go deeper and deeper into the entire Brandenburg-Prussian constitutional and administrative history, which goes back to the epoch of colonization, and I had to follow it from there up to the present. But also political history, in a specific sense, was not to be neglected. For the Prussian State, it is especially clear and understandable that internal arrangements were dependent on the tasks that sprang out of the international political situation. As it was, during the fifteen years that I directed the special periodical devoted to Prussian history, I also took a not insignificant part in the work of the Association for the History of the Mark Brandenburg. This was something like a historical commission interested in the sphere of provincial affairs, but at the same time, it was active also in general state history.

Nevertheless, I do not wish to say that Prussian history is my specific field of interest, as it is not the subject of my professorship at the University. It was due more to an external cause and request, which I felt that I should not turn down when in the last years, I began working on a short and compact history of Prussia to appear in 1915 for the five-hundred year anniversary of the Hohenzollern. This was not really a part of the main task that I have set for myself to fulfill as a scholar.

From the beginning, the real goal that I had in mind for my scientific efforts was a general comparative constitutional and administrative history of the states in the modern world, particularly of the Latin and Teuton nations. In this direction, I felt that the great life work of Ranke allowed for and needed supplementary work. Thanks to the suggestion of my honored teacher George Waitz, in my early years, I realized how important for this purpose a systematic study of law and political science is. On the whole, Prussian history would be a paradigm to me for the formation of the modern state and for the changes it underwent. Here, I could gather my own experiences in public life so that this whole field could be analyzed clearly. While pushing forward in many directions, here, I could hope to win a deeper and sharper understanding for the individuality of other state structures of similar or of a different type. Therefore, I occupied myself with Austria, Spain, The Netherlands, Switzerland, single Italian states; above all with France, England, America, the Scandinavian lands; and also with Hungary, Poland, Russia, and other single exotic states at least insofar as this is possible without a knowledge of the language of these countries. Out of these studies, and over a period of time in which I had special lectures dealing with single, especially important countries, I gradually built up my greater lecture on the general constitutional history of the modern peoples. This had been the chief object of my university teaching, and within a reasonable amount of time, I hoped to form it into a book. Through many years of work, I was convinced that a comparative treatment of the political and social institutions of the different peoples belonging to the cultural circle of the western Christian world would give fruitful results, indications of which here would lead me on too far. Some of these results can be found in the historical and political essays published by me, and in a pair of new publications. In these studies, it occurred to me to explain the present out of the past, to understand the present life of the western peoples and states (individually as well as a part of the international community) as the result of a great process of the development that proceeds from rather similar circumstances and continues in rather similar phases. On one hand, the consequences of different situations and conditions of living lead to a progressive differentiation of development and the individuality of peoples and states works out to be ever sharper. On the other hand, however, especially in modern times, intellectual communication brings about a gradual equalization so that the common types of modern cultural life in the areas of public and social institutions appear unmistakably clear. It is not enough to explain the individuality of the state out of the peoples' spirit (*Volksgeist*); for the most part, this is also a product of history. And also from another side, I would like to speak of conformity to laws in this development only in a very limited sense. They rule, if not unconditionally, in the lower more vegetative functions of the economic and social life of the people. In the higher regions of the political consciousness and deed, however, freedom and necessity are connected in a unique manner. This is true also for those who have in mind especially the institutions that are characteristic for humanity, and the lives of nations and that are the subject of the humanities (*geisteswissenschaftlicher Betrachtung*).

Nevertheless, it seems to me to be possible and necessary to bring the results of a comparative historical consideration of the lives (*Staatslebens*)

APPENDIX

of the modern nations into a systematic unity as historians and jurists have tried to do continually, and as I have tried to do continually in my courses concerning general political science (*Allgemeine Staatslehre*), based on an historical foundation. The categories of Aristotle will always have their worth, but for the new world of states, they do not go far enough. Working in the spirit of his methods, we must master new material. By studying constitutions in a comparative historical way, we must obtain a typical picture of the modern state in its common features (*gleichförmigen Grundzugen*); its tendencies of development; and its individual arrangements. We must also search for the causes that underlie the separate types of individualities (*Individualitäten*).

Thus flows my historical efforts in the field of political science. I am inclined to see political, social, and economic sides of the lives of peoples, which in the modern world cannot be separated from church affairs, as the real area of work for the historian—a universal cultural history, but one that in a wider sense seeks to bring together and to explain expressions of life of the human race as one great total picture. This task I am prepared to leave to the called and uncalled representatives of a universal science, to the genius of the future that will one day master it. For this task, I offer my work only as a modest preparatory work in the limited area of my own knowledge.[1]

---

1. Translated by Leonard S. Smith from the *Sitzungsberichte Der Koeniglich Preussischen Akademie Der Wissenschaften, Jahrgang* 1914, 744–47.

Epilogue
Teaching the Idea of History and Historicism as a Method for Writing a History Paper

For this presentation, "Teaching the Idea of History and Historicism as a Method for Writing a History Paper," each of you will receive two handouts. One is called "A Typology of Western Historiography," which consists of three "ideal types" or models: (1) An Ideal Type or Model of Classical Historiography, (2) An Ideal Type or Model of Christian Historiography, and (3) An Ideal Type or Model of Modern Historiography. Each of these models is based on Otto Hintze's ideal-type methodology and was developed and used in my history classes at California Lutheran University from the late 1970s to 1998 and later became the framework for the book *Religion and the Rise of History: Martin Luther and the Cultural Revolution in Germany, 1760–1810* (Eugene, OR: Cascade Books, 2009).

The second handout is a sheet of nine quotations, three from each of the three main periods of Western historiography, that I want to discuss with you today. The original purposes of these quotations were to provide a group of students and other groups a brief introduction to my book, my typology, and to what R. G. Collingwood called "The Idea of History." Secondly, in the year 2009, I first realized that I could combine this twenty-five minute discussion with the twenty-five minute writing assignment presentation that I gave to all my students in my "World Civilizations" discussion sections in the 1980s and 1990s. Here, I informed them how this brief research paper had to be a history paper, what this meant, how I would assist them in writing a good paper, and the standards that I would use in grading their papers. Formally, I called this presentation "Historicism as a Method of Teaching Students How to Write a History Paper." Thus, in the year 2009,

Epilogue

I realized that since I was probably the only college or university professor in the world who was using Otto Hintze's brilliant definition of historicism as a method for teaching first-year college and university students how to do history and how to write a history paper, the two presentations should be combined and should be published.

Let's start this discussion with the first sentence of Herodotus (ca-495–425 BCE), "the father of history." First of all, what is the significance of the first clause in this passage for the whole history of history? How many of you know what the Greek word is for the word that is translated here as "researches"? Why is this word, *historia*, translated here as "researches"? The reason for this is simple, for here Herodotus was simply saying that these were his researches, inquiries, investigations, or searches for the truth. The use of this word, its implications, and its connection with this first great artistic work of Greek prose, marks the beginning of history, for history is first and foremost a form of inquiry concerned not with "what gods and men have done" but—in the words of Herodotus in this paragraph—"what men have done."

When Herodotus used the phrase, "the great and wonderful actions of the Greeks and Barbarians," what kind of language is this? Right. This is epic language, and in this work Herodotus was imitating Homer, and at the same time, creating a new kind of epic: a prose epic.

Good start. Now let's go to the quotation from Thucydides (460–400 BCE). What main point would you make from this quotation? Good. With Thucydides, one can see an emphasis on evidence, on the basic procedure of the historian to interpret the evidence, and the linking of the procedure of the historian with the object of the historian: to interpret the evidence in order to present "a true picture of the events that have happened." Here we can see the historian's idea of truth, for historians are concerned with "factual truth" or with facts and events that can be established on the basis of rational and painstaking investigation of evidence existing here and now.

What does this quotation show about the attitude of Thucydides toward the stories of poets and their accounts of ancient times? Right. Does anyone here know the ancient Greek word for "poet?" A poet was a *mythopoios* or literally a "myth maker." What do we mean today when we speak of an age of "mythopoeic" thought? Basicallly, it was an age before Herodotus and Thucydides when the poets were the teachers of the Greeks, when myths were stories about god and men, and when myth was the highest form of truth. Thus, especially in this paragraph one can see a clear departure from mythopoeic thought.

Now, let's look at the quotation from Polybius (ca. 198–117 BCE). Here you can see that by this time, history has not only become a particular kind of inquiry and literature with its own name and that the persons who practice this kind of writing are called "historians," but also that Polybius believes that he has created a new kind of history. What are the words he uses for his new and superior kind of history? Right, general or universal history. It is very, important for the idea of history, however, that Polybius used the words *historia katholike*, which meant universal history. But like R. G. Collingwood, however, I believe that it is best to call this "oecumenical" history and reserve the term "universal history for the new kind of Christian historiography since the time of St. Augustine.

All of this quotation from Polybius is important, but how many of you were taught that history should be both useful *and* delightful? By the time of Polybius, rhetoric had become the key to a classical education, and history was commonly regarded as a branch of rhetoric. From the time of the Greek and Roman historians to the nineteenth century, history was commonly regarded as the most useful branch of rhetoric, for its function was to teach success. To be successful in life, it is necessary to have good examples to follow and bad examples to avoid. This is what history taught, but its examples and stories were also meant to entertain. Thus, as I pictured, portrayed, and summarized for you through my "Ideal Type or Model of Classical Historiography" that was handed out to you, Greek and Roman historiography was epic, humanistic, rational, and didactic.

Now, would you please look at my second ideal type, "An Ideal Type or Model of Christian Historiography." One of the most brilliant and useful aspects of Collingwood's *The Idea of History* was his analysis of Christian historiography. In his introductory sentence to a section called "Characteristics of Christian Historiography," Collingwood stated: "Any history written on Christian principles will of necessity be universal, providential, apocalyptic, and periodized."

Although this is a very sharp and strong sentence, and although Collingwood does not call these four characteristics an ideal type or model, in effect he created a very useful historical model for understanding and teaching Christian historiography from the time of St. Augustine to the Enlightenment and especially to the time of Voltaire.

Epilogue

To illustrate these four characteristics, let's look at the three quotations from this long period of time. The first quotation is from St. Augustine's *Confessions*. It is also a short one that we can easily read out loud together. Good. What is the main single idea, word, and concept that St. Augustine is illustrating in this passage and in this model "life writing" for the entire Christian epoch of Western historical thought? Right. But for more than twenty years, when I asked first-year college or university students this same question, each year the number of students who could come up with the word "providence" became fewer and fewer. The most common answer that I received was the word "predestination." And, at this time, my usual answer to this was that predestination is about going to heaven or hell and not about how or why you came to be here at this university.

The next quotation is from St .Augustine's *City of God*, an enormously influential book for the entire Christian era through the eighteenth century. Will you now read it and also the third quotation from this Christian era of Western historiography?

The third quotation from this era contains the opening lines of the first volume of a huge work (65 volumes) that was written by a large number of English scholars, that was called *An Universal History from the Earliest Account of Time*, and that was published from 1736 to 1765. One of the fascinating aspects of this encyclopedic work was the way these scholars sought to combine sacred and profane history, for while the first volume was a sacred history that began with "the Creation" and a discussion of the best date for this event, the other volumes were profane accounts of all parts of the world. For me, the quotation that you just read is the most beautiful fusion of Classical and Christian historiography that I have ever seen.

How many of you have been taught or believe that "History is without doubt the most instructive and useful as well as entertaining part of literature?" How many of you have been taught or believe that through the study of history, "every judicious Reader may form prudent and unerring Rules for the Conduct" of your life, "both in a private and public Capacity"?

Now, I want you to read the four characteristics of my ideal type or model of modern historiography. During the years from 1760 to 1810, especially in Germany and at the University of Göttingen, history gradually came to be regarded as a *Wissenschaft* or science, or as an organized body of knowledge with its own methodology. It was also at this time that the word *"Beruf"* gradually came to mean a "profession" rather than a "calling," and

Epilogue

when the words "individuality" and "*Entwicklung*" or development became basic concepts in Germany.

It was not until the work and the time of Leopold von Ranke, however, that history really became a fully professionalized *Wissenschaft*. The quotation from the preface of his first work that you have on your sheet of quotations, is still famous, for the words *"wie es eigentlich gewesen,"* soon became the most famous slogan for the new kind of professional historiography that he, more than anyone else, created and best represented; for here you can see a clear departure from the didactic characteristic of Western historiography to this time. For Ranke, history was both a science and an art, and no historian has ever written more great histories—both as research and as art—than he.

Now I am ready to begin my more formal presentation, a presentation that begins with the two quotations from Otto Hintze (1861–1940). Would you please look at them while I read them to you, for this is now the "historicist" part of this "classroom" presentation and—hopefully—my main contribution to the idea of history for future generations.

A Typology of Western Historiography
An Ideal Type or Model of Classical Historiography

1. *epic* because war and politics were the proper subject of this new kind of prose epic, and because Greek and Roman historians emphasized the greatness of events rather than their individuality or uniqueness;

2. *humanistic* because Herodotus created a way of seeing and presenting human events juxtaposed in time, and because in contrast to the mythopoeic literature prior to Herodotus and in contrast to the theocentric historiography of the Christian epoch, Greek and Roman historians were concerned not with the actions of gods and humans but with "what men have done";

3. *rational* because the word *historia* was a Greek word that meant "research, inquiry, investigation," or "establishing the truth," and because the main concern of Greek and Roman historians was to investigate the meaning and coherence of events in terms of the purposeful action of statesmen, military leaders, and other influential men;

4. *didactic* because after Thucydides, history came to be regarded as a branch of rhetoric and as an art that provided good examples to follow and bad examples to avoid; and because it was taught in the schools only for the purpose of providing rhetorical examples and not for the purpose of showing how things came to be.

Leonard S. Smith, *Religion and the Rise of History*, 4–5

An Ideal Type or Model of Christian Historiography

1. *universal* because the Judeo-Christian tradition is based on the words, "In the beginning God created the heavens and the earth" (Genesis 1:1), and because Christian historians sought to deal with the whole course of history in time and space;
2. *providential* because events were ascribed not to the wisdom of human agents, but rather to the working of providence or the hand of God in determining their course;
3. *apocalyptic* because Christians found revelation and meaning in the course of events through the life of Christ, and because they looked forward to the end of time, a last judgment, and eternal rest with God;
4. *periodized* because once this one universal course of events was divided into two main periods focusing on the life of Christ, it was natural to find lesser epoch-making events marking the beginning and end of other periods, each with its own characteristics.

Leonard S. Smith, *Religion and the Rise of History*, 16–17

An Ideal Type or Model of Modern Historiography

1. *professional* because history is written mainly by university professors who teach history for a living and who dominate the *Beruf*, calling, or profession called history;
2. *scientific* because historians believe—or act upon the assumption—that history is a *Wissenschaft*, a science or discipline, a method of understanding, and a mode of thought that can be taught and learned through a modern system of apprenticeship called the doctor of philosophy (PhD) and the *Habilitation*;
3. based on the concept of *individuality* because historians use the analogy of the individual person or life-unit in forming collective individualities, and because they are trained to look for the individual, the distinctive, and the unique in whatever human object or subject they study;
4. based on the concept of *Entwicklung* or *development* because these are the words historians use in constructing a meaningful, connected narrative based on a perception of time and on the analogy of the life-process of a single human being.

Leonard S. Smith, *Religion and the Rise of History*, 102–3

Quotations for a Typology of Western Historiography

"These are the researches of Herodotus of Halicarnassus which he publishes, in the hope of thereby preserving from decay the remembrance of what men have done, and of preventing the great and wonderful actions of the Greeks and Barbarians from losing their due meed of glory; and withal to put on record what were their grounds of feud."

—Herodotus, *The Persian Wars* 1:1

"Yet anyone who upon the grounds which I have given arrives at some such conclusion as my own about those ancient times, would not be far wrong. He must not be misled by the exaggerated fancies of the poets, or by the tales of chroniclers who seek to please the ear rather than to speak the truth. Their accounts cannot be tested by him; and most of the facts have passed into the region of romance. At such a distance of time he must make up his mind to be satisfied with conclusions resting upon the clearest evidence which can be had."

—Thucydides 1:21

"There is this analogy between the plan of my History and the marvelous spirit of the age with which I have to deal. Just as Fortune made almost all the affairs of the world incline in one direction, and forced them to converge upon one and the same point; so it is my task as an historian to put before my readers a compendious view of the part played by Fortune in bringing about the general catastrophe. It was this peculiarity which originally challenged my attention, and determined me on undertaking this work. And combined with this was the fact that no writer of our time has undertaken a general history. Had any one done so, my ambition in this direction would have been much diminished. But in point of fact, I notice that by far the greater number of historians concern themselves with isolated wars and the incidents that accompany them ... For indeed, some idea of a whole may be got from a part, but an accurate and clear comprehension cannot. Wherefore we must conclude that episodical history contributes little to the familiar knowledge and secure grasp of universal history. While it is only by the combinations and comparison of the separate parts of a whole,—by observing their likeness and their difference,—that a man can attain his object; can obtain a view at once clear and complete; and thus secure both the profit and the delight of History."

—*The Histories of Polybius* 1:4

"You applied the spur that would drive me away from Carthage and offered me enticements that would draw me to Rome, and for your purpose you made use of men whose hearts were set upon this life of death, some acting like madmen, others promising me vain rewards. In secret you were using my own perversity and theirs to set my feet upon the right course. You knew, O God, why it was that I left one city and went to the other. But you did not make the reason clear to me or to my mother."

—St. Augustine, *Confessions* 5:8

"The education of the human race, represented by the people of God, has advanced, like that of an individual, through certain epochs, or as it were, ages, so that it might gradually arise from earthly to heavenly things, and from the visible to the invisible."

—St. Augustine, *City of God* 10:14

"History is without doubt, the most instructive and useful as well as entertaining part of literature; more especially, when it is not confined within the narrow Bounds of any particular Time or Place, but extends to the Transactions of all

Quotations for a Typology of Western Historiography

Time and Nations. Works of this nature carry our knowledge, as Tully [Cicero] observes, beyond the vast and devouring Space of numberless Years, triumph over time, and make us, through living at an immense Distance, in a manner Eye-witnesses to all the events and Revolutions, which have occasioned astonishing Changes in the World. By these Records it is that we live, as it were, in the very time when the World was created; we behold how it was governed in its infancy, how overflowed and destroyed in a Deluge of Water, and again repeopled; how Kings and Kingdoms have risen, flourished, and declined, and by what Steps they brought upon themselves their final Ruin and Destruction. From these and other like events occurring in History, every judicious Reader may form prudent and unerring Rules for the Conduct of his Life, both in a private and public Capacity."
—*An Universal History* . . . (1747–1768), 1:V

"To history has been assigned the office of judging the past, of instructing the present for the benefit of future ages. To such high offices this work does not aspire: It wants only to show what actually happened [*wie es eigentlich gewesen*]."
Leopold von Ranke, "Introduction to *The Latin and Germanic Nations*,"
The Secret of World History, 58

"History can have as its possible object everything dealing with human culture in relation to a perception of time. The concept of the individual totality is, of course, crucial to determining an object of historical study; and I would suggest that the only decisive criterion is its comprehensibility as a life unit [*Lebenseinheit*]. The defining of objects of historical study, is in my opinion, an act of intuitive, not rational, thought. The historians thinking here is not logical but analogical. The concept of individuality underlies this analogical thinking."
—Otto Hintze, "Troeltsch und die Probleme des Historismus,"
Gesammelte Abhandlungen, 2: 337

Quotations for a Typology of Western Historiography

"What we call historicism is a new, unique, categorical-structure of the mind [*des Geistes*] that began to arise in the West in the eighteenth century and achieved authoritative currency in the nineteenth, particularly in Germany, though not in Germany alone. It is characterized by the categories of individuality and development, which postulate a view of historical reality based on the analogy of the life-unit [*Lebenseinheit*] and the life-process [*Lebensprozess*].

—Otto Hinze, "Troeltsch und die Probleme des Historismus," *Ges. Abh.*, 2:342

Bibliography

Antoni, Carlo. *From History to Sociology: The Transition in German Historical Thinking.* Translated by Hayden White. Detroit: Wayne State University Press, 1959.
Beiser, Frederick C. *Enlightenment, Revolution, and Romanticism: The Genesis of Modern Political Thought 1790-1800.* Cambridge: Harvard University Press, 1992.
———. *The Fate of Reason: German Philosophy from Kant to Fichte.* Cambridge: Harvard University Press, 1987.
———. "Hegel's Historicism." In *The Cambridge Companion to Hegel,* edited by Frederick C. Beiser, 270-300. Cambridge: Cambridge University Press, 1993.
———. "Historicism." In *The Oxford Handbook of Continental Philosophy,* edited by Brian Leiter and Michael Rosen. Oxford: Oxford University Press, 2007.
———. *The German Historicist Tradition.* Oxford: Oxford University Press, 2011.
Bendix Reinhard. "Bureaucracy." In *International Encyclopedia of the Social Sciences,* edited by David L. Sills, 2:206-19. New York: Macmillan, 1968.
———, ed. "Introduction [to Section D]." In *State and Society: A Reader in Comparative Political Sociology,* edited by Reinhard Bendix, 152-53. Translated by Hans Eberhard Mueller. Boston: Little, Brown, 1968.
———. *Max Weber: An Intellectual Portrait.* Garden City, NY: Doubleday, 1960.
———. "Otto Hintze." In *International Encyclopedia of the Social Sciences,* edited by David L. Sills, 6:366-68. New York: Macmillan, 1968.
Büsch, Otto, and Michael Erbe, eds. *Otto Hintze und die Moderne Geschichtswissenschaft: Ein Tagungsbericht.* Einzelveröffentlichungen der Historischen Kommission zu Berlin beim Friedrich-Meinecke-Institut der Freien Universität Berlin 38. Berlin: Colloquium, 1983.
Covensky, Milton. "Otto Hintze and Historicism: A Study of the Transformation of German Historical Thought." PhD diss., University of Michigan, 1954.
Dilthey, Wilhelm. *Einleitung in die Geisteswissenschaften: Versuch einer Grundlegung für die Studium der Gesellschaft und der Geschichte.* This is volume 1 of Wilhelm Dilthey's Gesammelte Schriften. (Unfortunately, this subtitle does not appear on the title page of the English edition of Dilthey's *Introduction to the Human Sciences,* Selected Works 1. Edited by Rudolf A. Makkreel and Frithjof Rodi. Princeton: Princeton University Press, 1989.)
Dorn, Walter. *Competition for Empire 1740-1763.* New York: Harper, 1940.
Erbe, Michael. "Otto Hintze und seine Sicht der Entstehung des neuzeitlichen Beamtentums." In *Otto Hintze und die moderne Geschichtswissenschaft: Eine Tagungsbericht,* edited by Otto Büsch and Michael Erbe, 87-94. Einzelveröffentlichungen der

Bibliography

Historischen Kommission zu Berlin beim Friedrich-Meinecke-Institut der Freien Universität Berlin 38. Berlin: Colloquium, 1983.

Gawthrop, Richard. Review of *Religion and the Rise of History: Martin Luther and the Cultural Revolution in Germany, 1760–1810* by Leonard S. Smith. *American Historical Review* 116 (2011) 1211–12.

Gerhard, Dietrich. *Old Europe: A Study of Continuity and Change, 1000–1800*. Studies in Social Discontinuity. New York: Academic Press, 1981.

———. "Otto Hintze: His Work and Significance in Historiography." *Central European History* 3 (1970) 17–48.

———. "Otto Hintze: Personlichkeit und Werk." In *Otto Hintze und die modern Geschichtswissenschaft: Ein Togungsbericht*, edited by Otto Büsch and Michael Erbe, 3–18. Einzelveröffentlichungen der Historischen Kommission zu Berlin beim Friedrich-Meinecke-Institut der Freien Universität Berlin 38. Berlin: Colloquium, 1983.

Gilbert, Felix. *A European Past: Memoirs, 1905–1945*. New York: Norton, 1988.

———. "German Historiography during the Second World War: A Bibliographical Survey." *American Historical Review* 53 (1947) 50–58.

———. "Otto Hintze und die moderne Geschichtswissenschaft." In *Otto Hintze und die moderne Geschichtswissenschaft*, edited by Otto Büsch and Michael Erbe, 195–208. Einzelveröffentlichungen der Historischen Kommission zu Berlin beim Friedrich-Meinecke-Institut der Freien Universität Berlin 38. Berlin: Colloquium, 1983.

———. "Preface." In Otto Hintze, *The Historical Essays of Otto Hintze*, edited and translated by Felix Gilbert, v–vii. New York: Oxford University Press, 1975.

Hartung, Fritz. "Otto Hintzes Lebenswerk." In *Gesammelte Abhandlungen* I, edited by Fritz Hartung. Leipzig: Koehler & Amelang, 1941.

Hexter, J. H. *Doing History*. Bloomington: Indiana University Press, 1971.

Hintze, Otto. "Antrittsrede des Hrn. Hintze." In *Sitzungsberichte der Königlich Prerussischen Akademie der Wissenchaften*, 1914.

———. "Antrittsrede des Hintze." In *Gesammelte Abhandlungen* I. 3rd ed.

———. "Calvinism and Raison d'Etat in Early Seventeenth-Century Brandenburg." In *The Historical Essays of Otto Hintze*, edited and translated by Felix Gilbert, 88–154. New York: Oxford University Press, 1975.

———. "The Commissary and His Significance in General Administrative History: A Comparative Study." *The Historical Essays of Otto Hintze*, edited and translated by Felix Gilbert, 269–309. New York: Oxford University Press, 1975.

———. "Der Beamtenstand." In Gesammelte Abhandlungen II.

———. "The Formation of States and Constitutional Development." In *The Historical Essays of Otto Hintze*, edited and translated by Felix Gilbert, 157–77. New York: Oxford University Press, 1975.

———. *Gesammelte Abhandlungen*. Edited by Fritz Hartung, 3 vols. Leipzig: Koehler & Amelang, 1941.

———. *Gesammelte Abhandlungen*, vol. 3. Edited and introduced by Gerhard Oestreich, 2nd enlarged edition 1967.

———. "Max Weber's Sociologie." A review of Max Weber, *Grundriss der Socialokonomik, III. Abteilung Wirtschaft und Gesellschaft*, 2 half volumes. Tübingen: Mohr/Siebeck, 1925. In GA II.

———. "Military Organization and the Organization of the State." *The Historical Essays of Otto Hintze*, edited and translated by Felix Gilbert, 178–215. New York: Oxford University Press, 1975.

BIBLIOGRAPHY

———. Review of *Max Weber: Ein Lebensbild* by Marianne Weber. In *Gesammelte Abhandlungen* II, 150–51.

———. "Roscher's politische Entwicklungstheorie." In *Gesammelte Abhandlungen* II, 3–45.

———. *Soziologie und Geschichte*. In *Gesammelte Abhandlungen* II.

———. *Staat und Verfassung. Gesammelte Abhandlungen* I. 2nd enlarged ed. Göttingen: Vandenhoeck & Ruprecht, 1962.

———. "The State in Historical Perspective." In *State and Society: A Reader in Comparative Political Sociology*, edited by Reinhard Bendix, 154–69. Boston: Little, Brown, 1968.

———. "Troeltsch and the Problems of Historicism, Critical Studies." In *The Historical Essays of Otto Hintze*, edited and translated by Felix Gilbert, 368–421. New York: Oxford University Press, 1975.

———. "Troeltsch und die Probleme des Historismus." In *Gesammelte Abhandlungen* II, 323–73.

———. "Typologie der ständischen Verfassungen des Abendlandes." In *Gesammelte Abhandlungen* I, 120–39.

———. "Wesen und Verbreitung des Feudalismus." In *Gesammelte Abhandlungen* I, 84–119.

———. "Wesen und Wandlung des modernen Staats." In *Gesammelte Abhandlungen* I, 470–96.

Hughes, H. Stuart. *Consciousness and Society: The Reorientation of European Social Thought 1890–1930*. New York: Vintage, 1961.

Iggers, G. *The German Conception of History*. Middletown, CT: Wesleyan University Press 1968.

Kocka, Jurgen. "Otto Hintze, Max Weber, und das Problem der Burokratie." In *Otto Hintze und die modern Geschichtswissenschaft*, edited by Otto Büsch and Michael Erbe, 150–88. Einzelveröffentlichungen der Historischen Kommission zu Berlin beim Friedrich-Meinecke-Institut der Freien Universität Berlin 38. Berlin: Colloquium, 1983.

Lehman, Harmut, and James J. Sheehan, eds. *An Interrupted Past: German-Speaking Refugees in the United States after 1933*. Publications of the German Historical Institute. New York: Cambridge University Press, 1991.

Meinecke, Friedrich. *Die Entstehung des Historismus*. Friedrich Meinecke Werke 3, edited by Carl Hinrichs. Munich: Oldenbourg, 1865.

———. *Erlebtes 1862–1901*. Friedrich Meinecke Werke 8. Leipzig: Koehler & Amelang, 1941.

———. *Historism: The Rise of New Historical Outlook*. Translated by J. E. Anderson, revised by H. D. Schmidt. London: Routledge, 1972.

———. *Machiavellism: The Doctrine of Raison d'Etat and Its Place in Modern History*. Translated by Douglas Scott, with an introduction by W. Stark. New Haven: Yale University Press, 1957.

———. *Strassburg / Freiburg / Berlin 1901–1919*. Stuttgart: Koehler, 1949.

Meisner, Otto. "Otto Hintze's Lebens Werk (27, August 1861–25, April 1040)." *Historische Zeitschrift* 164 (1941) 66–90.

Neugebauer Wolfgang. "Otto Hintze und seine Konzeption der 'Allgemeine Verfassungsgeschichte der neureren Staaten.'" *Zeitschrift für historische Forschung* 20 (1993) 65–96.

Bibliography

Nipperdey, Thomas. "Preussen und die Universität." In *Nachdenken über die deutsche Geschichte: Essays*, 140–55. 2nd ed. Munich: Beck, 1986.

Oestreich, Brigitta. "Hedwig und Otto Hintze: Eine biographische Skizze." In *Geschichte und Gesellschaft* 11 (1985) 397–419.

Oestreich, Gerhard. "Die Fachhistorie und die Anfange der sozialgeschictlichen Forschung in Deutschland." *Historische Zeitschrift* 208 (1969) 320–63. Reprinted in Gerhard Oestreich, *Strukturprobleme der frühen Neuzeit: Ausgewählte Aufsätze*, edited by Brigitta Oestreich, 57–95. Berlin: Duncker & Humblot, 1980.

———. "Otto Hintze's Stellung zur Politikwissenschaft und Soziologie." In Otto Hintze, *Gesammelte Abhandlungen* II, *7–*67. Berlin, 1962.

———. "Otto Hintze: Tradition und Fortschrift." In *Strukturprobleme der frühen Neuzeit: Ausgewählte Aufsätze*, edited by Brigitta Oestreich, 127–41. Berlin: Duncker & Humblot, 1980.

Rand, Calvin G. "Two Meanings of Historicism in the Writings of Dilthey, Troeltsch, and Meinecke." *Journal of the History of Ideas* 25 (1964) 503–18.

Roscher, Wilhelm. *Politik: Geschichtliche Naturlehre der Monarchie, Aristokratie, und Demokratie*. 2nd ed. Stuttgart: Cotta, 1893.

Rubanowice, Robert J. *The Crisis in Consciousness: The Thought of Ernst Troeltsch*. Tallahasse: University Press of Florida, 1982.

Schieder Theodor. "Die deutsche Geschichtswissenschaft im Spiegel der Historischen Zeitschrift." *Historische Zeitschrift* 189 (1959) 1–105.

———. "Der Typus in der Geschichtswisssenschaft." In *Staat und Gesellschaft im Wandel unserer Zeit*, 172–87. Munich: Oldenbourg, 1958.

Smith, Leonard S. "Otto Hintze's Comparative Constitutional History of the West." PhD diss., Washington University, 1967.

———. *Religion and the Rise of History: Martin Luther and the Cultural Revolution in Germany, 1760–1810*. Eugene, OR: Cascade Books, 2009.

Troeltsch, Ernst. *Der Historismus und seine Probleme, Erstes Buch: Das logische Problem der Geschichtsphilosophie*. Gesammelte Schriften 3. Tübingen: Mohr/Siebeck, 1922.

Winkelmann, Johannes. "Introduction." In *Max Weber's Soziologie*, edited by Johannes Winkelmann. Berlin: Ducker & Humblot, 1956.

Yasukata, Toshimasa. *Ernst Troeltsch, Systematic Theologian of Radical Historicality*. American Academy of Religion Academy Series 55. Atlanta: Scholars, 1986.

www.ingramcontent.com/pod-product-compliance
Lightning Source LLC
Chambersburg PA
CBHW071451160426
43195CB00013B/2082